Michael Luck

THIRD EYE AWAKENING, KUNDALINI AWAKENING AND CRYSTALS FOR BEGINNERS

A Complete Guide to Open Your Third Eye, Expand Your Mind through a Spiritual Growth and Discover the Healing Power of Crystals

Table of Contents

Introduction 5

Chapter 1.   The Third Eye 9

Chapter 2.   Opening your Third Eye 31

Chapter 3.   Psychic Abilities and the Third Eye 35

Chapter 4.   What is Kundalini Awakening? 46

Chapter 5.   Types of Awakenings 56

Chapter 6.   Kundalini Yoga 73

Chapter 7.   Kundalini vsMeditation 84

Chapter 8.   What are Crystals? 93

Chapter 9.   Choosing Your Crystal 108

Chapter 10.   Crystals And Chakras 124

Chapter 11.   30 Crystal to Know 133

Chapter 12.   Basic Meditation 164

Chapter 13.   Kriya Yoga - Prana and Apana 185

Chapter 14.   Kundalini Exercises 198

Conclusion 216

Introduction

Have you ever felt like you're stuck in a rut? Do you ever feel like you're missing something? Maybe you feel like something's holding you back. Maybe you feel like you're not living your life to the fullest. Third Eye Awakening is an energy that has been manifesting in the world since the beginning of time. It has never been stronger than it is right now and is being felt by more people than ever before. If you feel like you're experiencing Third Eye Awakening, you're not alone.

The third eye, also known as the inner eye or sixth chakra, is a spiritual concept referring to a speculative invisible eye that provides perception beyond ordinary sight. It is associated with the pineal gland, which is a pea-sized endocrine gland in the vertebrate brain. The third eye is the energetic center of the body, and it's located between the eyebrows. It's linked to intuition and prophecy, and if you're feeling energized around the third eye area, it's because you're tapping into your intuition and psychic abilities

Kundalini is a Sanskrit word meaning "coiled up" or "coiled like a serpent." It's the primordial energy of the universe and the life force of every living being. It's located in our spine's base and is the most powerful energy source in our body. I've been practicing yoga and meditation for a long time and have always felt that there was more for me to learn from these practices. I also felt that there was something more for me to learn from other cultures and other modalities.

Kundalini Awakening And Crystals techniques are the most powerful techniques to raise your vibration and to transform your life. It is known as one of the most powerful techniques to raise your vibration. These techniques will take you on a journey into the depths of the universe.

When we are born, each of us has a unique aura, a unique life signature in life. Your chakra system is part of that unique signature. As we grow, our chakras can absorb energy received from our experiences in life and everything that we learn. They absorb this knowledge by reading your energy and taking it into your self-understanding system. When you go through difficult situations in your life, such as traumas, constant fights, and discouragements, your chakra system will react to these stimuli and block the flow of energy so as to prevent the flow of negative energy to your whole body. If they are not unblocked, this will result in creating a false identity that will hide who you truly are.

There are various chakra systems, but the most known in the West is the seven chakra system. Those seven chakras, along with their corresponding colors and locations of each one:

- Root Chakra: Red - found at the base of the spine
- Sacral Chakra: Orange - found just below the navel
- Solar Plexus Chakra: Yellow - found at the stomach area
- Heart Chakra: Green - found at the center of the chest
- Throat Chakra: Blue - found at the base of the throat
- Third Eye Chakra: Indigo - found at the forehead between the eyes
- Crown Chakra: Violet - found at the top of the head

It may seem impossible that energy moves through the chakras or discs to some people, but this belief has endured for thousands of years, and many have benefited from learning and taking care of their chakras. Yogas are examples ofAyurvedic medicine, where illness is viewed as the blockage of energy in one or more chakras. Acupuncture is also based on helping the energy flow through our bodies since blocked energy will lead to pain and disease.

Throughout this book, we will analyze everything you need to know about the Third Eye and awakening it to gain all the benefits associated with it.

Chapter 1.   The Third Eye

The third eye is a term reserved for a physical and spiritual part of the body. In its physical form, the pineal gland is a gland located at the top of the spine that connects with the brain. Physiologically speaking, this endocrine gland has many functional purposes within the body. It is often referred to as the third eye outside of scientific circles. If you were to look someone squarely in the face, the pineal gland would sit just above both eyes, right in the center, like another eye, hence its name.

The pineal gland produces hormones like melatonin and serotonin, which play a big role in regulating sleep patterns and improving the overall mood. Without this gland, the body would not recognize normal fluctuations in light, making it difficult to fall and stay asleep in a normal pattern. In the bigger picture, the body would not be able to recognize summer from winter, aside from the temperature change. The pineal gland exists in most vertebrate animals, and therefore, keep the entire ecosystem running on the same clock, based on sunlight.

While the pineal gland's functional purposes are generally known, there has always been a bit of mystery surrounding the small gland. Early scientists assumed that this gland was highly important because of its location within the brain. The tiny gland sits dead center between the right and left hemisphere of the brain, and deep under its tissues, almost like the rest of the brain's function is to protect this small piece. Please think of the meat of a walnut encapsulated tightly in its outer shell.

The pineal gland's ideaof being the third eye in the spiritual sense is much more powerful than the pineal gland's physical properties. Many cultures have long believed that this third eye holds the key to life, and that is no small task. The power of the third eye goes above and beyond recognizing light patterns and channeling energy and light, which drives the body.

The power of prophecy, seeing the future, is also associated with a strong pineal gland. The idea is that a clairvoyant person has a very strong connection with the universe. This knowledge transcends time and allows you to sense things that will happen in the future. It is not necessarily as depicted on television. A clairvoyant does not necessarily see things happening in the physical sense but through energy.

Many people also see energy in a physical sense. There are auras of energy that surround each and every living thing. The energy emitted takes many different shapes and colors, depending on positive and negative energy. The third eye communicates with the universe's energies in this way, and learning to recognize these energies is important for ultimate guidance. Many say that negative energy is depicted as red, while positive energies are much lighter, white, or shades of green. You would not willingly walk into a room full of people with red auras if you could see them, would you? Likely not, but the average person only sees the room full of people and enters anyway.

Opening the spiritual eye means seeing the world in a new light, recognizing the connections between your inner energy and that of the universe, and sensing or seeing the energy all around us. Throughout history, the third eye has been celebrated as the utmost in knowledge, education, and higher being. Having a well-functioning third eye means having a connection with the higher energy, a God, Gods, or any combination thereof, depending on the classic culture.

We can see the impact of the third eye throughout history in art. Early on, the pinecone became synonymous with the pineal gland. In fact, the name pineal comes from 'pine.' The pinecone had graced this planet with its existence long before any other plant species on earth. It is ancient, and its perfectly aligned spiral structure represents energy and perfection in the deepest senses. Looking through artworks throughout the centuries, even dating back to the ancient Egyptians, we see pinecones. It is meant to symbolize divine wisdom and our spiritual soul.

Hindu and Indian cultures also use the pinecone to depict the highest enlightenment and wisdom of their gods. In Hindu culture, all of the gods are depicted in art and lore with pinecones, with Shiva being the most prominent. Indian culture depicts the god Kundalini, with an awakened third eye, bringing wisdom, love, and joy.

The third eye isn't restricted to Eastern cultures. It also spans from Mexico and the Central American region, and even with the

Native Americans indigenous to North America. While the traditions and rituals to harness this third eye's power vary, the outcome is the same. People throughout history have recognized the third eye as the window to their soul, and the connection to their universe.

With all of this discussion of the third eye's history, it is important to remember that modern man also possesses the pineal gland, the third eye, and a spiritual connection. As time wears on, it seems that humans have become much less connected with their spiritual selves, and the power of the third eye is waning. The importance of spiritual connection often falls through modern medicine and factual evidence for what ails us.

We need to remember that the spirit is wholly in charge of our physical being and that the energy of the universe is boundless and never-ceasing. We cannot be happy and healthy with a spirit that is unwell. Therefore, it is vital to nurture our third eye and our spiritual connection, just as we treat our bodies well. We need to embrace our spiritual culture and reconnect to be whole, and functional, and human.

If you are looking for science, there is that too. It has been found that the calcification of the pineal gland can be the cause of many physical and mental ailments. This calcification happens when minerals and other elements build up around the gland, causing a decrease in function. Calcification presumes that calcium is the major problem, but other elements, like fluoride and chlorine, also increase the calcification process.

As we age, calcification increases, disrupting sleep patterns and creating overall stress within the body. This stress can manifest itself in several ways, including weight gain, chronic disease, and a dysfunctional immune system. Studies have also linked calcification to Alzheimer's disease and memory loss in general.

This gland also produces DMT, a chemical that has been associated with so-called hallucination and loss of consciousness. This chemical allows us to dream, to enter another world. The idea of this being a hallucination is a fallacy created by man to explain the phenomenon. Those guided by their spirit can recognize that the loss of worldly consciousness and entrance into a higher plane is their soul transcending the body and time as we know it.

Many people have vivid, very real dreams, while others don't. It is believed that the lack of DMT creates a dreamless sleep, and the soul remains stuck within the confines of the body. It is unable to escape and collect wisdom from the universe. Many say they can also find this transcendence through the practice of meditation, a very advanced skill.

These changes in function and behavior can be directly related to a decrease in melatonin DMT and serotonin but have also long been described in a spiritual sense as losing one's connection with the spiritual universe.

The energy of the universe is all-knowing and helps guide our lives. Being connected helps ensure a steady path in all aspects of life, as the universe gives you the insight and wisdom you need via energy patterns. For example, when you are in a good place, you are surrounded by positive energy, which your body is attracted to. Your third eye has a keen sense of encroaching negative energy, and if you are truly guided by it, it can be avoided.

Do you feel connected to the universe? Do you have a keen sense of your surroundings? Do you feel you make good decisions? It is hard to know if the path that you are on is the right one, but there are usually clues. If you feel as if you have no destined path in life or keep making choices that lead you to negativity, you are likely not in touch with your third eye.

This can be a helpless feeling. Imagine that you have cast offshore in a boat with no oars and no sails. The boat aimlessly floats, with no way of steering through deep swells and rogue waves. If this sounds like your life, it is time to reacquaint yourself with your spiritual being. All of the positive energy and wisdom you need lies dormant within you. It is only a matter of harnessing that power to make positive changes in your life.

We can improve this spiritual connection in several ways, all of which will be described throughout this book. Learn to decalcify your pineal gland, reconnect with your true self, and with the endless energy of the universe. Your life is special, and you are meant to live a meaningful and productive life. Now is the time to do it.

Wellness of the Third Eye

If your pineal gland is out of sorts, problems will manifest themselves throughout the body, mind, and spirit. Paying attention to this tiny gland and keeping it healthy is important to your overall health and wellness. Continuing to neglect, it means new problems will continue to emerge over time.

Physical effects: With modern science taking a hold on our society, let's discuss the scientifically proven, physical effects of a calcified pineal gland, or third eye. Calcium and fluoride are the two biggest calcification culprits, sticking to and creating a hard layer over the gland, decreasing its function. One of the biggest changes will be the output of melatonin, the hormone most well-known for proper sleep and maintaining circadian rhythm.

Other factors can affect the pineal gland as well, including chlorine, environmental chemicals like pesticides, and artificial sweeteners found in an abundance of foods. Basically, any substance that is foreign to the body, and has no way to manage can affect the pineal gland.

The direct effect will cause trouble falling and staying asleep, especially compared to your normal pattern. A good indication of calcification is an abrupt change in your normal sleeping pattern that cannot otherwise be explained. Keep in mind that increases in stress, caffeine too close to bedtime and a poor sleeping environment can all contribute to this problem.

Melatonin is also responsible for a number of other functions, including proper onset of puberty in children. If the pineal gland is affected by excess fluoride in the diet, delayed puberty can occur, which will affect the course of growth and reproduction. In adulthood, a calcified pineal gland can also spell trouble for conceiving a child and overall sexual capabilities. Problems with sex drive and fertility have clear links to decreased melatonin caused by a dysfunctional pineal gland.

Melatonin is also an integral part of the body's natural defense against free radical damage. Simply put, free radical damage occurs when cells are exposed to environmental toxins, oxidation, and stress. These factors stress and cause damage to cells, leading to cell death. This break-down of cells means that your overall function decreases, and the aging process quickens. Melatonin is on the front lines of helping cells battle free radicals and conserve healthy cells.

If you are feeling generally sluggish and tired, even with adequate rest, there is a good chance your pineal gland is calcified, and this process has already begun. Depression is also another common symptom, as serotonin, your 'happy hormone' is greatly affected as well. While depression can be situational, if you are feeling low most of the time and nothing seems to help your depression, it could point to your pineal gland as the culprit.

Emerging science has also shown that the pineal gland has ties to cancer, hypertension and other chronic diseases that were once thought to be independent of each other. As research continues, we find that all systems within the body are connected, and hormonal imbalances, much like the one happening in a calcified pineal gland can be the true root causes of chronic disease.

Perhaps one of the most interesting developments from a calcified pineal gland is excessive cravings for alcohol. While the cause is still being explored, it is well documented that calcification and alcoholism correlate. This implies that pineal gland calcification can actually be a root cause of alcoholism and can certainly hinder the treatment process.

Emotional effects: A dysfunctional pineal gland can significantly impact emotional health. There is some fascinating science explaining how environmental factors like magnetic fields and toxins can alter our mental function through our pineal gland.

As we discussed earlier, the pineal gland is not exclusive to humans; it is found in all vertebrate animals. In other mammals, the gland functions as a compass to orient the animal in time and space. It works off of positive and negative energy, magnetics associated with the earth's atmosphere. For example, birds know where and when to fly south for the winter because of changes in light (melatonin) and by following the earth's magnetic pathways. Studies have shown that changing the magnetic field around the bird will cause disorientation.

This is a fascinating fact because it can be applied so easily to humans. We would be foolish to think that the same gland birds have is not functioning the same way in humans. Perhaps this is why centuries of culture have named the pineal gland the source of knowledge, wisdom, and guidance. This gland is literally responsible for our orientation within the world, both physically and emotionally.

Further studies insist that changes in electromagnetic fields, like that occurring during a solar flare, actually increases the incidence of depression and suicide in humans. The vast changes in magnetics disorient the pineal gland, causing decreases in melatonin and serotonin, increasing depression.

While changes in magnetics can be a supporting factor, it is well known that environmental effects of improper diet, chemical exposure, and environmental toxins are more likely causes of pineal trouble. Long-term exposure to any number of these elements causes calcification and suppressed hormones, specifically serotonin.

As we know, suppressed mental and emotional capacity affects the outcomes of life. When we are tired from a lack of restful sleep, we are short-tempered and ineffective. It will hinder our ability to work, creating stress within our jobs. Concentration wanes with lack of sleep, making even the simplest tasks most difficult.

When you are tired, it seems the only thing to think about is getting to sleep, making it through the day, scraping by, waiting for your head to hit the pillow. Once it does, the illusion of sleep may appear, but doing so may not be possible. Melatonin has not been produced, and therefore, you are stuck with insomnia. This imbalance causes this cycle of fatigue and insomnia, and over time, can be debilitating and downright annoying.

It is really no wonder that with our hectic work schedules, exposure to heavy metals and toxins, poor diets, any of us are even alive. Many of us muddle through life, hoping to feel better someday, yet stuck in a depression that keeps us from even having the energy to try to make positive changes. This is depression and poor mental health.

Spiritually

Followed directly behind our emotional demise is our spiritual one. The third eye is seen as our pathway to seeing the world and the universe around us. Energy naturally flows in and out of it, guiding us and bringing joy and light to our lives. It is the pathway for our inner selves, our souls, to shine through. A calcified pineal gland forms a shell around our third eye, hindering its ability to see and be everything it needs.

Our spirit can easily become suppressed, buried away within that shell, making it nearly impossible to live our best lives. Imagine that your inner self at its best creates a huge aura around you that shines bright, attracting and grabbing positive energy and guiding you forward. Imagine its suppression as that bright light being just a small ember tucked away inside your mind. On the outside, your spirit doesn't show, and you wander aimlessly, hoping for direction.

Most of us know from experience that feeling depressed or tired really hinders the spirit. It is very hard to feel enlightened, free, and boundless when we barely have enough energy to get through the day. There is no room for creative ideas, big dreams, and there is certainly no drive to go after it without a true spiritual backing.

There is no doubt that a calcified pineal gland will affect your overall quality of life. Now that you have seen the different possible side effects of a dysfunctional third eye, it is time to take steps to fix it.

The Power and Benefits of Opening the Third Eye

There are numerous benefits to opening or awakening the sixth chakra, your Third Eye. It should come as no surprise that having a more relaxed and healthy mental state can also result in a healthier physical state. Six of the main benefits or powers that one may experience from opening their third eye are increased overall health and wellness, increased psychic power, astral travel, increased creativity, more vivid dreams or lucid dreaming, and the frequent experience of positive space order. Third Eye Awakening is one of the most important practices when talking about awakening the seven chakras.

Overall Health and Wellness

The most commonly experienced health benefit by those who have experienced Third Eye Awakening is eliminating stress and anxiety from their lives. Opening your Third Eye results in an increased sense of relaxation and belonging within the universe that will minimize or eliminate the feeling of stress in your life. Stress has been listed as a factor that increases one's risk of developing obesity, diabetes, asthma, Alzheimer's, and other physical illnesses (if one suffers from one of these conditions already, stress can worsen the illness). Since research has proven the link between stress and numerous health conditions, it is important to eliminate stress from your life; you can experience relief from stressors through Third Eye Awakening.

Increased Psychic Power

Humans used to rely on the very primal instinct of intuition to survive. In today's society, we often refer to this as being our "gut feeling" or explain it as "something doesn't feel right". This feeling results from our mind receiving very subtle, undetectable cues from our body's five senses. The cues our minds receive from our senses, in this case, often do not have concrete evidence to back them, though our minds know to interpret them as positive or negative signs for making a decision. By opening the sixth chakra, you make it easier for your mind to decipher these instinctive signals and increase the frequency of feeling that intuition will guide these decisions. Awakening your Third Eye offers the psychic benefit of great relaxation, universal consciousness, and heightened empathy feelings.

Astral Travel

Astral Travel is often described as "dreaming while awake," and many consider this concept to be like having an out-of-body experience. Astral travel is your mind's ability to experience your surroundings without being limited to your physical body. Astral travel allows your soul to be free from your physical body to travel the universe freely. Everyone is born with some minute amount of psychic ability, and if you do exercises to strengthen your psychic abilities, anyone can become capable of astral projection. When the astral body is projected from the physical body, the two remain connected by the astral cord (or silver cord), which can stretch to almost infinite length and cannot be severed (except the occurrence of death).

Increased Creativity

Third Eye Awakening is also extremely beneficial in reenergizing your senses of imagination and creativity. Opening your Third Eye allows you to problem-solve with ease since your mind had been relaxed and open to all the available possibilities and solutions. The awakening of the sixth chakra enables you to be more receptive to greater details, which results in an increased sense of creativity and an increase in the frequency of vivid dreams.

Vivid Dreams/Lucid Dreams

The sixth chakra's biological name is the pineal gland, and the pineal gland is responsible for producing and regulating the hormone melatonin within our bodies. Melatonin is responsible for our sleep/wake cycles. By opening your Third Eye, we relax the pineal gland, which often results in a better, deeper sleep. Deeper sleep sessions can often lead to more vivid dreams and vivid dreams more frequently as the relaxed mind is then more receptive to greater detail. Lucid dreams are different from the experience of vivid dreams, though they tend to be quite vivid and life-like as well. Both vivid dreams and lucid dreams are common occurrences to a fully awakened Third Eye, though lucid dreams are often described as dreams in which you maintain control of what happens within your dreams and the infinite possibilities that exist there. Awakening the Third Eye results in the ability to view infinite possibilities in the dream realm, but you will also be able to view the infinite possibilities in reality through the opening of the sixth chakra.

Space Order

The concept of space order is widely discussed as one of the common results of Third Eye Awakening. This can be described as an idea similar to "you get what you give," as space order is similar to the universe's form of Karma. By opening the Third Eye, you give off more positive energy. In turn, you become a sort of magnet for receiving more positive energy in the form of positive events, experiences, and meetings with other individuals.

Chapter 2.   Opening your Third Eye

You can do a few exercises to get ready for and begin to open your third eye; once opened, your third eye has many benefits, such as helping to regulate your overall mood, sleep, and energy levels.

Some people become sensitive to different sounds or tones; often, people find low tones soothing and higher tones uncomfortable. Often people taste in music alters because of their new "sight."

Light sensitivity sometimes affects people as well, often people become more sensitive to bright light, and some find they see a much fuller spectrum of colors. Some people also develop a craving for more sunlight on their skin.

Sunlight exposure helps to kick start the pineal gland and also stimulates the mind. This is the neurotransmitter that is responsible for mood and energy levels. To produce melatonin, you need the exact opposite, making it very important to avoid light at night to utilize your third eye fully.

Before the invention of artificial light, our ancestors were used to having a cycle of about 12 hours of darkness and 12 hours of light. Our bodies and system are programmed for this cycle. Sleeping with the lights on, even if only a very small amount of light can disruptive and affect your pineal gland's ability to produce melatonin. With any form of light, it will keep making serotonin. If it is necessary to have a night light, it should be a red light, not blue or green. So always try and sleep in total darkness. When you sleep in total darkness, it allows the pineal gland to increase its production of melatonin and stimulates the production of pinoline and DMT (Dimethyltryptamine) as well as opening the third eye.

Sungazing is one exercise that is very controversial and also can be quite dangerous. Some people use it to activate their pineal gland; it should only be attempted within the first 15 minutes of sunlight and the last 15 minutes at the end of the day. The idea is to do for only a few seconds and this is important, only a few seconds, look directly into the Sun. Probably a much better idea is to just spend a good part of each day in the sun, you will allow your skin to produce vitamin D and feel and look much healthier. And at the same time stimulate your pineal gland safely.

Our eyes need to be exposed to indirect sunlight every day for several hours, if you wear sunglasses this means you are not getting the sunlight you need as sunlight reflected by the retina stimulates the pineal gland. If you cannot spend several hours each day in sunlight, you should install full-spectrum light bulbs to bring these benefits indoors year-round.

You can do some simple exercises to prepare for opening your third eye, such as breathing chanting, tapping and laughing, and smiling.

Breathing through your nose is recommended, slowly breathe in and hold for a few seconds, then slowly breathe out, the idea is to breathe down into your stomach, and your chest area should not inflate. Breathing deeply helps to activate the pineal and pituitary glands.

Using a magnetto stimulate the pineal gland, place a magnet on your skin at a point just slightly above and between your eyebrows. Leave it there for several hours each day when first starting to open your third eye. This is also a good way to help your body to become alkaline.

The reason people trying to open their third eye chant such things as "OM" is because this chanting stimulates the pineal gland by causing the tetrahedron bone in the nose to resonate. Another method is to press your tongue to the roof of your mouth. This helps to activate your pituitary gland, and also with its physical and chemical connections, it causes the pineal gland to be activated as well.

Laughing and smiling both have the effect of reducing stress levels and relaxing the body. This triggers the release of endorphins that promote feelings of wellbeing and happiness. Relaxation has the effect of increasing the blood flow; this can amplify the hormones that activate the pineal gland.

Chapter 3. Psychic Abilities and the Third Eye

One particular chakra, the third eye chakra, requires a little more focus than the rest because it is connected with the "sixth sense" and psychic powers. Therefore, a separate chapter dedicated to the Ajna Chakra makes sense here to enhance your ability to handle Kundalini Awakening when it happens.

To reiterate, the third eye chakra is located at the center of the forehead, right between the eyes. The color associated with this energy center is indigo or royal blue. It is the seat of our psychic powers. It regulates and controls our psychic powers so we can receive and transfer information to the realms beyond the planes of human consciousness. It is the seat of our internal intuition, and when fully developed, can read the past, present, and future accurately. A person with a well-developed Ajna Chakra can interact and get guidance from the spirit realm and from loved ones who have crossed over.

The Ajna Chakra is also an effective and powerful manifestation tool. We can use it to visualize our dreams and hopes and harness the universal power to manifest them in our life. When we visualize our dreams, it is more than just our imagination working. It sees our desires through our inner eye.

Interestingly, the Ajna Chakra is closely connected to the solar plexus chakra or our "gut feeling." When these two energy centers are aligned with each other and work synchronously, our life can turn out meaningful and fulfilling. The synchronized energy of the two centers can help us understand and harness our intuitive powers to overcome our challenges and difficulties easily.

With an open and balanced third eye chakra, we have improved clarity and focus along with a powerful intuition.

Here are basic tips to activate, strengthen, and balance the third eye chakra and the energy it holds:

- Practice visualization and meditation regularly, both guided and simple breathing types.
- Try to include royal blue and indigo into your life, whether in the clothes you buy, the colors you paint, the jewelry you choose, or anything else.

- Holding or wearing gemstones like Lapis Lazuli, Tanzanite, Amethyst, Apatite, and Labradorite help to enhance your meditation experience.

- Work with Tarot Cards and other forms and conduits of oracles.

- Massage the area of your third eye with our essential oils like myrrh, sandalwood, etc.

- Don't forget to give daily thanks to your third eye and its power to help you lead a happy, fulfilling life.

Opening the Third Eye Chakra

Keeping the third eye open and energy flow as free-flowing as possible is essential to not only harness your spiritual powers but also to return safely and sanely from those realms beyond human consciousness, a common outcome of Kundalini Awakening. These strategies have known to work magical wonders to open the third eye and keep its energy balanced and unblocked.

Cultivate Silence - Learn to foster the silence of your mind. For an average human, the mind is a cacophony of thoughts and ideas that threaten to take our world by storm. Not only this, but these thoughts also create a lot of noise in our minds. Our ability to hear and interpret the messages that come to us from the higher and subtler realms get lost in the noise.

The third eye chakra can go to that "in-between" space to collect and get guidance and messages from the other world's spirits. In the presence of noise, you cannot hear the messages. Therefore, you must cultivate silence of the mind and learn to handle overwhelming thoughts.

You can use various ways to calm and silence your mind, including meditation, indulging in your favorite hobby or art, or simply sitting calmly in the midst of nature doing nothing but observing the surrounding beauty.

Hone your intuitive powers - we all are endowed with intuitive powers. The problem is these powers need to be continuously honed and sharpened for them to be effectively used. Not using them regularly dulls our intuition, and we get disconnected from our inner voice that receives and passes on messages from the outer world. The sharper your intuition is, the more powerful your third eye chakra becomes.

Here are simple ways to connect with and hone your intuition:

First, recognize how and when your intuition speaks to you. Usually, intuition is not loud and clear like a human voice. Instead, it sends subtle messages through slow-moving or flashes of imagery. Often, you will talk with your intuition, wondering how to get clarity about the received message.

Sometimes, the messages come in goosebumps, an uncomfortable feeling in the gut, a sour taste in your mouth, or a sense of inexplicable relief. Often, the messages could come as an emotion. For example, you intuitively like or hate someone you've just met. This could be your intuition, sending you a message about this person.

Just be alert to subtle forms of messages that your body and mind send you. To do that, you must connect with and talk with your inner voice. With practice, you will realize that you can easily catch on to the subtlest of hints that your intuition is trying to give you.

Try to connect with your intuition daily - Keep aside a dedicated time to connect with your intuition daily. Give time and effort to your intuitive powers and see what they are trying to tell you. This is especially important when you have to make a critical decision. However, to ensure you can understand your intuition's language, you must talk with it every day.

Take small decisions, too, after consulting with your intuition. It could be something as seemingly mundane as which dress to wear each morning. Stand in front of your wardrobe for a little while and ask your intuition which dress would suit you best today. Then, calm your mind, and look out for signs and signals it might be sending to you. Like this, try to connect with your intuition daily.

Write down what you felt or experienced when you tried connecting with your intuition. Don't leave it to your memory, at least in the initial stages of your learning experience. Write down what you felt, your thoughts, and everything else when you sat down each day and connect with your intuition. The more practice you get, the better your skills will become.

Meditate as often as you can; the deeper your connection is with your intuition, the easier it will be to read and interpret its messages. Meditation is an excellent tool to deepen your connection with your intuitive powers. Meditation teaches you to clear your mind and recognize the subtle impulses and signs that your intuition is trying to give you.

And finally, **learn to trust yourself and your intuitive powers.** The more faith you have in your powers, the better outcomes you will get. Trust yourself because no one loves you more than you do. No one wants to see you happy and successful more than you do.

Build Your Creativity Skills

Each one of us is born with creativity. It is up to us to nurture, nourish and develop it to achieve our full potential. Creativity is a useful tool to eliminate rational fears and crutches that hold you down when you are, in reality, powerful to soar high in the clouds.

When your rational mind is relegated to the background, then the mental chatter also reduces, helping to achieve the calmness needed to communicate with your intuitive powers. When you can calm that part of your mind that wants to take charge of your life, you are effectively opening up numerous opportunities for yourself. Your third eye chakra has increased space to unfold, grow, and blossom.

How can you nurture your creativity? Here are tips to help your creativity grow and blossom:

- Invest your time and energy in hobbies and activities that energize you and make you happy. Learn a new craft or art. It is not important to be perfect in what you do. The trick is to let your inspiration flow through your mind into your hands. Be ready to be surprised when you allow your creativity to flow unhindered.

- Experiment with creativity. You need not have a perfect plan. Just do anything that requires your creativity to flow through. For a simple example, just buy yourself an adult coloring book, and experiment with colors. Or make a palette of watercolors and simply splash them around on a piece of paper and observe the results. Or put on some music and dance to it as if no one is looking at you.

- Get sufficient nourishment for your body through nutritious food, restful sleep, and a good amount of physical activity.

- Invest in yourself. Do something once a week that is only for you. It could be something as simple as a visit to the local art gallery or sipping a cup of morning tea by yourself, or an afternoon curled up in bed with your favorite book, or anything else. This alone time will give you a deep sense of calm and allow you to connect with yourself and your intuitive powers.

- Spend some time with nature. Take a walk in the park. Or take a hike to a place close to your home. Look for and find an opportunity to spend time with nature.

Ground Yourself to Soar Fearlessly - It is an ironic truth that we must plant both our feet firmly on the ground to soar fearlessly. In the same way, to open our third eye, our root chakra should be strong and robust, giving you the needed sense of stability and strength with the support of which you can soar fearlessly. Your root chakra forms the firm foundation over which you can build your life that takes you on wondrous flights outside the human realm. The root chakra is what brings you back home.

Also, the information that comes into our body and mind when our third eye is opened could be unfamiliar, unusual, and difficult to digest for common minds. Therefore, you must first energize and empower your tangible body and mind, and only when you are ready can you tackle the power of the subtle universe.

Chapter 4.   What is Kundalini Awakening?

Kundalini is the extremely strong psychic force that resides within each and every one of us. It's known as Shakti, and it's the life force that propels our inner self forward. It is usually represented as a coiled and sleeping snake, and when we are born, it is dormant at the base of the spine. Kundalini Shakti's snake unwinds and ascends through the Sushumna Nadi in the middle of the spinal column as this force is stimulated and awoken. The Sahasrara, or crown chakra, at the top of the head, is its final destination. Kundalini Awakening occurs when Kundalini connects with our 7th chakra, causing the person to transcend into a heightened spiritual state.

The prana, or life force, contained in the food we consume and the air we breathe is consumed at a much faster pace when Kundalini yoga is practiced. The Apana, which is the energy of elimination or return, is a partner in this transformation. Tappa, or heat, is generated inside the navel center when the prana and Apana energies are combined. The Kundalini force is awakened when the heat from the tappa descends into the Muladhara chakra.

What is a Kundalini Awakening, and how does it happen?

When people begin to feel movement in their bodies, they will most likely feel a stirring of Kundalini energy. As the chakras are triggered, they can feel an energy change that makes their perceptions far more conscious. These moments, however, are brief and only last a few days. Kundalini awakening in its entirety is exceedingly unusual. It happens when all of the psyche's problems and knots have been confronted and resolved. As Kundalini energy surges up from the Muladhara chakra, it passes through the back of the spine and over the top of the head, finally landing in the 3rd eye chakra. The entire system has been changed and awakened at this stage.

Kundalini Awakening and Stirring Symptoms

Since the energy blocks that were part of the spiritual, mental, emotional, and physical bodies are largely responsible for the symptoms, each person's symptoms are special. When these blocks are struck, symptoms are usually felt. The signs will go away until they've been dealt with properly. Many common symptoms, however, are felt more commonly, including:

Periods of increased imaginatio

a flash of insight or wisdom into the complex workings of truth

Strange sounds, such as thunder, musical instruments, or buzzing, are heard internally.

Your senses are quickly overwhelmed.

Emotional mood swings that can be very serious

Orgasm may be caused by waves of bliss or pleasure.

Immediately recognizing and learning previously unknown pranayamas, asanas, bandhas, mudras, and kriyas

Cold sensations all over the body, as well as extreme heat or aches in the spine and chakras

A sensation of snakes or insects crawling over your body, especially along your spine

Jerking or shaking of the body that the practitioner is unable to manage

Lightning bolts or electricity inside the body are energetic sensations.

Itchy feet or hands are a normal occurrence.

How to Deal with the Signs and Symptoms of Kundalini Awakening

Symptoms will appear even if you have done personal spiritual work on yourself before beginning Kundalini yoga. The onion peel has so many layers that you won't know how far you have to go until you've been through them all. There will always be something that needs to be dealt with, let go of, or transformed.

When all of the above symptoms become unbearable, it's a sign that there are circumstances, feelings, or past traumas that need to be confronted so that they can no longer control you. If you get into the habit of letting go of the burdens you've been bearing, letting go of these stuff can become second nature to you, even though you've been holding onto them for decades. You'll find that you were carrying a lot more weight than you knew or were willing to admit. Sitting and meditating, as well as light pranayama, are two ways to get over the negative symptoms. Determine the location of your discomfort, whether physical or emotional, and perform a breathing exercise that focuses on the corresponding chakra. Meditation will often aid in the relaxation of the mind, allowing you to think more clearly. You can also be led to the answer if you will listen to your inner guidance and intuition.

It's important to note that if these symptoms appear, it means you're on the right track to cleansing your body in preparation for the Kundalini awakening. The obstacles will be hit and hopefully eliminated, allowing you to begin a new life filled with boundless ecstasy and bliss.

Reduce your practice time if you're noticing that meditation or pranayamas aren't making the unwelcome symptoms go away. You can be pushing yourself too hard at times.

It will take determination and perseverance.

During this process, however, you must pay attention to your body. Other things you can do in your day to help with the symptoms and your overall health

Kundalini's regular routine is to go for a long stroll. It will not only calm the mind, but it will also allow the body to work through some of the symptoms while relaxing the Kundalini Shakti. Tai chi is also a great exercise to implement because it will help you to stay grounded.

You are not dissolving the Kundalini energy when you ground yourself. In reality, it is bringing in the masculine aspect in order to balance and calm down the feminine Shakti energies that are felt through our nervous system. Grounding yourself will get your nerves back to normal function every time you feel stressed during a Kundalini session.

If the symptoms begin to intensify or vanish, you can investigate three aspects of your life: habits, diet, and lifestyle. Unbalanced or balanced Kundalini Shakti is caused by these two factors.

When it comes to practices, you can take a close look at the structure of the activities you're doing. Perhaps they require practice on a particular chakra, or the exercises require you to balance the feminine and masculine energies. If you discover that this solves your dilemma, keep making the improvements you've made and go with the flow. However, it often includes more than one aspect. When it comes to the lifestyle side, this can be a big deal. Pose the difficult questions to yourself.

• Should you engage in too much or too little spiritual practice?

• Is it possible for you to strike a comfortable balance between your activities and your everyday life?

• Do you work long hours at work and neglect your other commitments as a result?

• Is your job spiritually supportive of who you are as a person?

• Do your mates distract you from your spiritual concerns?

• Does your partner encourage or discourage you in your attempts to awaken Kundalini?

What If There Isn't Any Feeling?

If you don't have any of these Kundalini signs, what do you do? Maintain your Kundalini workout routine. They will most likely arrive in due time, but they might not be felt at all at times. It all comes down to how you handle the Kundalini awakening process. You would have an easier time than someone who lets their emotions run wild or has a narrow view and views about life if you can let go of things quickly and not let too many things bother you. All is relative. Only know that if any symptoms do arise, you will have a clearer understanding of why they are occurring.

Chapter 5.   Types of Awakenings

Kundalini Awakenings can be quite confusing if you do not realize what is occurring to you. There is much misinformation, which can be easily looked up online, which is often misleading. Many times, someone feels they have gone through the awakening process, even though they are just going through the first stages.

In truth, many transformations happen throughout the process of the awakening process. Even though you may start experiencing instances in which are otherworldly or cannot be easily explained, it does not necessarily mean you have had a full Kundalini Awakening experience. It does not happen overnight, but you will start to see the signs. See where you are in the awakening process with this explanation of the different stages of Kundalini awakening.

Firstly, it is important; to be honest with yourself about what is happening with your body, mind, and soul. There are times that we try to put unexplained symptoms we are feeling into a brighter light. Know that even though you may be practicing the exercises for Kundalini, there may be underlying medical issues that you would rather categorize as part of the Kundalini awakening process when they are due to other causes.

It is also important to note that every person who goes through the Kundalini awakening process will experience something unique to themselves. There is no cut-and-dry set of experiences that you will be able to find, which exactly explains what you are going through. This is what makes each person unique. You will deal with deep-seated issues within you differently than another person, or your attitude about the awakening process and how it changes your life may go more positively than the next person. Just understand it is a process, and only you can work through it in your own way.

The Awakening process is basically that you are having a second birth while discovering this dormant energy available to you your whole life. It will aid you in coming to know and understand your true nature within yourself, and there are many ways in which your new "gifts" will manifest themselves. Trust in the system and be kind and understanding with yourself as not all of the things you will come to understand are going to be pleasant. It is also helpful to think about the end goal of becoming your full authentic Self and that you becoming more awakened is a healing process. And it is very likely that once you are on the other side of this process, you will be able to help others.

The First Stage - Kundalini is Dormant

The first part of the process is that there has actually been no awakening of Kundalini Shakti. This is quite common as this energy has laid dormant your entire life. The tricky part of this part of the process is that you have had one or two enlightening experiences where you were overwhelmed with bliss and emotion that you feel you are now awakened. Honestly, it is not that easy.

You are likely in this category when you are first starting with the Kundalini exercises, even if you have been dutifully practicing for months. It will likely take hundreds of altered states of consciousness to reach enlightenment. This does not degrade the profound experiences you may have already experienced, but know that you have to dig deep to purify the body to the point of having the full Kundalini awakening occur.

This part of the process can be quite confusing due to the fact that we have a world of information at our fingertips on the internet. It sets someone apart as special when they say they have gone through this process, and it is all too easy to find someone else who is claiming they have become enlightened when they have just started the process. The intuition heightening, hearing ethereal voices or even your inner voice lets you know that you are on the right track, but this is not a full awakening.

So be wary when you read about someone who happens to be going through the same incidents as you and claiming they are enlightened and awakened. It is better to listen to your body and follow your intuition on such things. Also, you took the right step in getting this book because then you will be more educated on the fact, which is half of the battle.

You must realize that there are going to be altered states of consciousness that may happen by other means which will also bring about vibrations in the body, blissful sensations or feeling the illuminated. You need to discern the truth behind these feelings and not try to put all ethereal experiences in the category of being awakened. Just trust in the process and go with the flow of what is being presented to you instead of relying on other people to tell you what is going on within your body.

The awakening process is an extremely personal experience, which is not going to be a cookie-cutter version of what someone else who is going through the same exercises and experiences. Just know that most people will be found in the first stage, which is the most talked-about stage on the internet and in spiritual circles.

The Second Stage - Kundalini is Starting to Wake Up

The second stage, which is experienced by practitioners of Kundalini, will feel more intense as the coiled snake is going to start waking up

intermittently. This is going to result in more pranic energy being able to flow through your body, which results in the symptoms of Kundalini awakening. Again, this is a long process that will make an effort to make through to the end of being enlightened. At this stage, you will start to actually feel the changes that are occurring within your body because your awareness has been forced to look within. You may feel the benefit of the nadis becoming more cleansed and balanced. You may also feel surges of energy, which can be attributed to Kundalini, but this is not a full awakening. You are just at the threshold of the process.

What makes people so convinced that they have gone through the awakening process is that they may realize some of these changes within the body are permanent or even physical changes in appearance. It is hard to argue that something so profound is not a Kundalini awakening, but just stick with the Kundalini exercises, and you will see that there are other grander ways in which you will transform.

When you are in this stage of awakening the Kundalini energy, you will feel sensations that are not always pleasant. They may bring out physical or psychological pain or send you to a high and blissful state. Be understanding of yourself and do not judge. This is part of the process where every aspect of yourself is going to need examination. There is a lot of letting go and reevaluation with new eyes of things you may have experienced in the past.

It is best for your progress through the Kundalini awakening that you see things in a detached manner to objectively look at yourself. When you take away the power and emotions that these instances are bringing up, you are actively able to let go of these burdens you have been carrying. In turn, you will further purify your body so that the pranic energy and Kundalini are able to flow through nadis that once were clogged.

When you feel surges of energy or clarity run through you, which evenly subside, you show signs of going in the right direction for your personal Kundalini awakening. However, you have a far way to go yet. But this is not something to get discouraged about. Sometimes it takes years of dedicated practice to get the final result of absolute enlightenment.

The Third Stage - Kundalini Bestows Gifts

The third stage, which is, experienced further increases in the pranic energy, which is flowing through your nadis. There are even a lesser amount of people who are able to make it to this stage. If you have been working on the exercises and cleaning and recharge your chakras, you will get to this part of the process. Congratulations! Many people do not get to this part of the awakening process. This is due to the massive amount of work people accomplish with clearing and balancing their first three chakras, which is usually the hardest part of the process.

You may still think that you have experienced a full Kundalini awakening during this stage. This is because there are obvious signs that Kundalini has been awakened as you will start to feel "sparks" of energy flowing from the base of your spine all the way to the top of your head. In fact, this is called Pranotthana, and it is a temporary experience. It may last for half a second or even for days.

However, this energy subsides eventually.

This is where you can see your true progress within the process. When the Kundalini energy is able to go through your body, even for a short instance, you surely know you are doing things right. Keep up with your hard work; it will certainly pay off as you have made it through more than half the race. How much longer it takes is entirely up to you. In fact, Kundalini energy can become dormant again, even at this stage. You must continue to keep your nose to the grindstone and remind yourself of what goal you are going after.

Even during this stage, you will start to realize even more changes occurring within you. You will likely have moments of complete illumination or epiphanies. These are just guideposts to notice, continue to grow, and give confidence that you are on the right track. Always keep a humble heart, and be grateful for these instances in which you feel you are enlightened. Take them and learn from them. This information is given to you so you can use it to become closer to your true and authentic Self.

When you continue on with your Kundalini practices, these instances of Pranotthana will continue to occur, eventually more frequently, and become more intense. When you are allowed by

Kundalini to see all the truth in reality and your role within it, these are gifts that will continue to motivate you. You are getting closer to your end goal, and it is certainly not the end of the race just yet. This is the time to listen to your body and continue to push yourself to greater heights.

Even after the sensation of the "sparks" go away, the information, visions, and what you had possibly heard are going to stay within you. This information can never fade away. You need to use this knowledge to continue to look within yourself as this is your inner intuition guiding you through this process. Kundalini wants to reunite with its Universal Consciousness, and these experiences and information as gifts from Kundalini Shakti to help get you there.

It is also positive to note that when Kundalini can travel up through the chakras, she is doing her own cleaning of these chakras. After these experiences, the chakras will stay open, even partially. This continues to aid you in the process of having your total system balanced so that you can reach the 4th and final step: Kundalini Awakening.

The Fourth Stage - Full Awakening of Kundalini in 1st Chakra & The Accent

The truth is there are going to be very few people who make it to this stage of enlightenment. It is extremely rare. However, those that are determined, dedicated, and genuine in their path to connect with their true higher Self will reach this state of awakening. The individuals who make it through to this part of the process are in the same company as mahatma, great souls, Jesus, Buddha, and Krishna. Some would say it is within their destiny to make it to this awakened state.

Even those who start to experience the awakening of Kundalini have further work to do in their bodies. You will have fully awakened Kundalini Shakti, but she is only awakened within the first chakra, the mooladhara. When this occurs, there is a further process of Kundalini connecting fully with each chakra. This gradual climb occurs as if you were building a temple within your being and is a slow and arduous process.

During this stage, Kundalini stops shocking your chakras through the pranotthana experiences. She starts to work her way up slowly up each vertebra of the spine, ascending further when the body is fully prepared to continue rising. Of course, it is Kundalini Shakti's utmost desire to reunite with utter consciousness. This can only be done with completing the tasks you require, such as inner quality, values, freed mind, and proper virtues.

It is rare to find any person who has reached this enlightenment stage to speak about their experiences. Firstly, it is an extremely personal experience. Secondly, it has been documented that if they speak of their experiences or boast about what they have accomplished, they will lose the abilities they have gained. It is an experience that only should be shared in secret as it is your personal connection with the divine. It is not something that should be announced proudly to the entire world.

It is also very possible that Kundalini Shakti will not be able to rise any further than the 1st chakra. You must continue your inner work for it to continue to climb. Kundalini also can go back into a dormant state at this stage. However, when one gets to this point, they will likely have the mindset required to continue with the process. They have gotten this far already. They would consider it unfair to their true nature to stop when they are given the finish line.

One of the many powerful symptoms of reaching this stage of Kundalini awakening is that you are in the seat of consciousness during the day and night. That is, you are completely aware and awake, even while you are sleeping. Your world will seem like a lucid dream, but you know you are not dreaming.

When you are aware and connected to your divine spirit, you are in this stage of development. They are consciously living outside of their bodies.

People may not make it to this stage because Kundalini Shakti can put you through a type of death while you are still in your body. Since you live in this state of awareness, not associated with your body, you may go through what others would deem as a coma that could last over a week. You will not be taking in any food or water, but your spirit will be completely conscious. In this state, you will be receiving instructions from other fully awake beings of the nature of your purpose and responsibilities and what direction you need to take. If this state lasts too long, the physical body will die.

Chapter 6.   Kundalini Yoga

This type of yoga is an ancient science and art which deals directly with the expansion and transformation of consciousness. The end result after dedicated practice is the raising of Kundalini energy, which flows through the chakras. Through the combination of pranayama, bandhas, asanas, mudras, and mantras, there is a build-up pressure, which forces the Kundalini energy to be awakened to rise up through the body. In addition to these exercises, focused attention, projection, and visualization are key to acquiring specific effects.

When a person practices Kundalini Yoga, they are able to unite their consciousness with the Ultimate Consciousness when they practice daily. It is not a quick process, and much care needs to be taken to ensure that specific combinations of exercises are performed. Once a student starts to perceive the movement of energy outside, and within the body, they are able to consciously direct the flow of the pranic energy to unblock, clear, and awaken the chakras. In turn, they will be healing themselves and even others as they become one with the universal energies.

Kundalini yoga has been gaining popularity since the 1980s in the West since Yogi Bhajan brought over the teachings from India. He was considered a Kundalini master at the young age of 16. He first emigrated to Canada in 1968 and moved to Los Angeles, California to teach Kundalini shortly thereafter. His utmost goal was to make each individual holy, happy, and healthy. His non-profit organization named 3HO is still functioning today through his students as he passed away in 2004.

The typical traditional Kundalini yoga sessions include a balanced distribution of physical yoga poses, meditation, and breathing exercises. They also incorporate mantras into their meditations, which assist the newcomer in mediation with the silence, which is required for meditation. These mantras differ from other Sanskrit mantras which are commonly used in Sanskrit because they are usually from the Gurmukhi language.

The combination of different aspects of yoga practice is known as *kriya*, which translates to "action" from Sanskrit. A particular kriya will have a focus such as a physical, emotional, or mental health benefit. These can range from letting go of anger, discovering inner intuition, or eliminating health issues such as lower back pain or poor digestion. Some of these kriyas' names are Kriya for Conquering Sleep, Navel Adjustment Kriya and Kriya for Elevation.

Hatha Yoga

Known as the most popular form of yoga in the West, Hatha yoga focuses more on the physical practice of yoga than Kundalini. However, the physical practices were taken from Hatha yoga to be practiced in Kundalini yoga. People who practice Hatha yoga do not perform the mantras and pranayamas in their exercises.

Hatha yoga was born out of Tantric yoga practices and is believed to be approximately 5,000 years old. Swami Swatamarama wrote the first text, which was written about Hatha yoga in the 15th century. The core belief of Hatha is that enlightenment could be attained when you strengthened the connection with your physical Self.

The traditional practice of Hatha consists of some breath work or a short meditation in which they proceed with many different yoga poses. Some of the poses common to Hatha yoga are Warrior, Mountain, Child's, and Downward Dog pose. As the individual is practicing the yoga poses, it is a slow process marked by precision and striving to make the pose correct and perfect. It is not necessarily a fast-paced or physically demanding type of yoga; however, there are always exceptions.

In respect to Kundalini yoga, Hatha yoga share several of the same physical positions and breathing exercises. Sometimes a Hatha practitioner may even use some of the mantras which are used in Kundalini yoga. The largest difference between the two is how the yoga sessions are structured with Hatha yoga focusing on bettering the physical Self and Kundalini yoga's focus is on the spiritual experience, which can be felt inwardly. However, both types of yoga strive to increase awareness and flexibility, remove stress, and have a goal of becoming balanced in body, mind, and spirit.

Bhakti Yoga

This yoga style is understood to be the path to devotion, which is based on emotion and reality based on our emotions. Emotions are the root of the most intense experiences we have in our reality. Feelings are able to make us experience the highest highs and the lowest hells. They can unite people together for their lifetime or burn bridges without the thought of looking back. Certainly, everyone can agree that emotions are the number one intense experience that we can have as human beings.

The purpose of bhakti-yoga is to teach a way to control these intensely emotional experiences to live their lives for the better. The devotional path of bhakti teaches their students how to transform their negative emotions into more pleasing ones. The way they view life is through eyes of love. When you focus your mind on love and how it makes you feel, it can make everything in your life look that much brighter. It also plays on the Law of Attraction.

Being in a state of love also has a chemical effect on the brain. More dopamine is released into the brain when you are feeling love or remembering memories that are close to your heart. When you feel this way, you tend to ignore all the negative things in your life and around you.

Some people may think this is too much of an unrealistic way of viewing life. However, it is very detrimental to be bogged down with negative emotions of anxiety, anger, sadness, or stress. There needs to be a happy medium. However, bhakti yoga only focuses on this one aspect, whereas Kundalini yoga is much more profound on an internal and external level.

Gnana Yoga

For those who want to strengthen their intellect and mind, jnana yoga is right up their alley. However, this is not necessarily for the Harvard graduate. How we define intelligence in today's society, it is very ego-based and materialistic. True intelligence cannot be measured by test scores, complex thoughts, or big words. No, the real type of intelligence is not attached to a value or a particular outcome.

This type of intelligence is gathered in a particular way because of your awareness level of activities occurring around you. It brings about complete focus without getting wholly involved. You could say that jnana yoga's motto is "it is what it is" as they embrace this fact. It is a form of detachment as intellect disbelieves nothing and simultaneously believes in nothing.

Karma Yoga

There is a misunderstanding that there is good and bad karma. However, the truth of the matter is there is simply karma. The definition of karma is the use of the physical energy within your body. The belief in karma yoga is that a coiled spring is located inside of each of us which much be released during physical activity. If this spring is not released, there will be a buildup of energy with us which will need to be released. When this becomes the case, it causes people to become nervous and agitated.

During karma yoga, the eternal actions performed are expending the karma centered around this coiled spring. When energy is dispersed each day, it can be a liberating experience rather than entangling. The performed activities are not necessarily things that you want to do, but because they need to be done. The end result of this activity is that it causes a stillness within you that becomes your reality. It is not just an idea because it becomes your life.

Kriya Yoga

This type of yoga focuses on the emotions, mind, and body being external to you as they are not what defines you. Instead, they are your realities based on your experiences in life. Kriya in this sense if your energy is a reality experienced internally.

The motto which could be used for this type of yoga is that "everything happens for a reason," and it is not part of the practice to come to the bottom of the reasoning. However, the purpose of kriya yoga is to put trust in the process and open yourself up to the possibility that nothing can have an explanation in the physical world. This thought's reasoning is that the ego tries to explain everything as it assigns, meaning the insignificance and chaos of our individual lives.

They believe they are just energy which the use of a body and mind which helps to facilitate their experiences in this life. They are able to separate their physical experience of living from their energy. They want to understand the inner workings of the energy and soul within them.

Of course, when it comes to Kundalini yoga, all these yoga types are just smaller pieces to a larger puzzle. Kundalini digs deeper than any of the other types of yoga. It also much more physical and requires a great deal of dedication if you want to realize the true end goal of Kundalini - to have the coiled serpent rise through all of your chakras. The end result is the liberation and freedom from the confines of this bodily existence. It is surreal and unimaginable and quiet difficult to attain without guidance. However, there are steps that anyone can take to start on the path to enlightenment. In short, all other types of yoga focus on one central point within ourselves. Kundalini yoga makes you take apart each part of yourself to examine and polish or toss away parts of ourselves that do not mesh truly with who you are inside. There is simply no comparison. As long as you come to this path of yoga with sincerity and respect without expecting to experience actual awakening after doing it for a few months, then you are prepared to start.

Chapter 7.   Kundalini vsMeditation

The relationship between meditation and kundalini energy is very important. Meditation aims to clear the mind, letting thoughts roll by and not distract us from our one-pointedness. This clear-headed state is imperative to a successful kundalini working. We need a clear mind to focus our energy and attention on the task at hand. If we are distracted, we will not be able to engage our inherent energy. Without some sense of attentiveness, we will not be successful in our efforts to manipulate this energy.

Meditation's ultimate goal is to clear the mind and offer a sense of oneness. While we don't particularly need to be in this blissful state for a kundalini working, it helpsus understand this state. The most important factor that meditation can offer for our kundalini workings is a focused mind. If we can put aside all of our mundane thoughts and memories for enough time to focus our attention on our energy, we will be more aware of the kundalini progress and workings. This one-pointedness that meditation offers is incomparable to any other practice.

Meditation is unique in its ability to offer a sense of clarity for the mind. Simply sitting and breathing is safe and easy; it truly is remarkable how powerful such a simple exercise can be. When we sit down to meditate, we are, in essence, sitting to enter a different state of consciousness, blissful and comforting. These practices are crucial to any balanced lifestyle, and for kundalini, they are invaluable.

There are thousands of different meditation techniques, each of them with its specific use or traditions. As we explored above, it is difficult to find a solid definition for meditation, but overall its goal of achieving a truly clear mind is at the heart of any meditation exercise.

For our kundalini meditation, we must treat it similarly to kundalini yoga. You will not want to have a full stomach for these workings, and you will want to warm up a bit before beginning. We suggest doing some casual yoga and short breathing exercises before performing the following practice. You will not want to go from a normal state of consciousness and then try to jump right into a heightened one. We need to ease ourselves into these more advanced practices to ensure we do not have unwanted outcomes.

When we are approaching kundalini meditation, we need to learn from the master who brought kundalini to the west, Yogi Bhajan:

"Meditation is a process...At any time which is peaceful (the best is in the early morning time, before the dawn), you'll be surprised that in a couple of minutes, a lot of thoughts will start coming to you—the X-rated thoughts, the ugly, angry thoughts. If you let those thoughts pass by, this is meditation. All those thoughts that can pass at that moment of your life can never enter your subconscious mind, and they will not bother you again. This procedure of cleansing the mind is called meditation. It takes about three minutes to get those kinds of thoughts. And sometimes they continue to bug you for about half an hour. But, if you physically don't move, the mind becomes still. That is the foundation or the beginning of the meditative mind. Once your mind starts becoming still and not having any thoughts, you will feel cozy, and that coziness cannot be described even by me. All I can tell you is that it is very comfortable, it is very cozy, and you will want to do it again and again. But in the beginning, you cannot do it for a long time. Gradually, as you develop that coziness, this thought-hitting process becomes shorter and shorter."

There is a common misconception that when you sit down to meditate that your mind will quiet itself. This is misleading; the mind is so chaotic that it will not quiet itself easily. When we meditate, we look inward to discover that we are the listener to our thoughts. How can this be if we are just one person? This is duality, and to eliminate this duality, we must be in the present moment. If we can fully be here now, we can eliminate the distracting thoughts from our past or future. This is a very powerful state to be in, and meditation is the tool to get us here.

When we meditate, we will get distracted. It's inevitable. But we cannot give up on our practice. We must shed the distracting thoughts and not let them trip us up. When we do get distracted, we must realize this distraction and brush it off, continuing our practice from the start. This is not a failure, but a simple challenge, a bum in the path on our way to kundalini awakening.

Do not be discouraged. Even the most experienced yogis get distracted by the chaotic nature of the mind.

Meditation is a blissful and comfortable place that we can enter at any time and in any environment. This cozy and welcoming place is found through rigorous effort and dedication to the power of the present. This comfort stems from the oneness that accompanies expanded consciousness. Even when distracting thoughts arise, we must see them off. They will not hook their ugly thoughts onto you if you are attentive and one-pointed. Let them wash away on your breath.

Ignite the Kundalini

This exercise is designed to activate the kundalini energy through deep meditation. If you can attain this state of being, you can personally reach out and touch the kundalini energy, awakening it lovingly and gradually.

1. Sitting on the ground with legs crossed for the first five minutes, relax every muscle in your body. Imagine a white light is caressing you on the inside, releasing every problem, distraction, and trouble you have.

2. Let your body gently rock back and forth. This may be in figure-eight or side to side. Whatever is comfortable to you and comes naturally.

3. Let each vertebra in your spine be affected by the rocking motion of your body.

The energy will begin to flow upward from the bottom to the top of your head. This will loosen the Kundalini up so that she can rise completely out of the top of your crown chakra. During this time, keep your focus on the energy between your sexual organs and the base of your spine. Breathe the white light into this area, attempting to engage kundalini.

With this dedicated concentration, you will feel tingling energy along the base of your spine. It may even move upward. The more comfortable ad natural this experience is, the more likely kundalini will be awakened.

The moment you start to feel a rising of energy, stop the rocking and be completely still. Set the intention for your thoughts to slow down and eventually stop. Begin to relax into the calmness. Breathe slowly and deeply for five minutes. You will start to notice that your body is breathing on its own accord. Let this natural breathing cycle continue, and do not try to control it.

When you are completely relaxed into the stillness, resting deeply inside, relax into your spinal column, ensuring you maintain good posture. At this point, focus on the chakra energy starting at the root chakra. Engage this energy and move it up to the crown chakra, visualizing the colors as you go:

- Red – Root

- Orange – Sacral

- Yellow – Solar plexus

- Green – Heart

- Blue – Throat

- Indigo – Third eye

- Violet – Crown

Each chakra region will have a circular vortex and flooding color around it; move slowly through these energy centers as you guide the energy upward. As you approach the crown chakra, let the energy flow out of the top of your head and fall down all around you, then continue the process, starting with the root chakra.

This will form egg-shaped energy all around you. It will be a rainbow in color or golden white. Maintain this egg as you continue the exercise, circumambulating the body with energy and stimulating kundalini. This egg will be shifting in color as you continue this practice. Do not be distracted by the color; rather try and move it as it flows around you. Separate the colors and filter them through your body as you continue to manipulate the energy.

If you feel a burst of distinct energy pulse up your spine, you may have awakened kundalini. Everyone's experience is different, but overall this pulse will feel different from the energy you have been working with. Also, this energy may abruptly stop your meditational attention and take your focus to a different realm. You will know if/when this happens, it may be startling at first but do not be frightened.

As you continue, this exercise maintains the rainbow egg state for as long as possible. Your sense of time will change, and overall your perception will be heightened. Once you leave this state, you can contemplate your experiences and see if you can improve your practice for next time. Practicing this exercise multiple times a week is recommended. You may not be able to reach the same rainbow state each time, but do not be discouraged as you continue your path to kundalini awakening. You must be consistent and truly dedicated to awakening this serpent.

Chapter 8. What are Crystals?

We'll start our journey by coming to understand what crystals are from a scientific perspective. To the average person, a crystal is nothing more than a pretty rock. Likely that makes you wonder just how an inanimate object like a rock is going to help you heal. This is a normal reaction by most people and is probably one of the main reasons why so many are reluctant to recognize the healing powers hidden inside each of these precious gems.

Yes, crystals are indeed on the surface, just another type of stone, but each one is unique, and you won't find any other stone with the kind of properties it possesses. Every crystal has its own energetic properties that can be channeled in all sorts of directions. These beautiful rock formations can be used in thousands of different ways, many of which go far beyond mere decoration.

This is not just some spiritistic hype that only those with blind faith might believe. Few people realize that the world's first radios were only able to transmit their signals with crystals' aid. It is a scientific fact that we will discuss throughout the following pages of this book. While people see first their natural beauty and want to put them in the same company as they would diamonds and rubies, looking beyond the surface will reveal so much more.

- **What are Crystals and Where Do They Come From**

In scientific terms, crystals are simply a grouping of molecules and atoms. While they are hardened like a stone, each crystal has its own unique characteristics. First, they are formed from a variety of different natural materials on earth. Some are made from salt, and others come from other elements found in the natural world. Gemologists and geologists have a unique definition of a crystal. They describe it as a solid object with atoms that are organized in a repeating lattice pattern. While there are several different crystal patterns, we're only going to focus on those that can be used for healing. These are sometimes described as gemstones, minerals, or rocks.

Minerals: Not all minerals can be classified as crystals, but those that are, have a highly organized structure that is formed by the special way the atoms interlock together. As they grow, the variations of temperature and chemical composition that occur underneath the earth's crust throughout the eons of time it takes to form to give them their distinctive properties.

Rocks: Rocks are stones formed from several various minerals, but all rocks can be considered crystals.

Gemstones: These are those rocks that have been cut and polished so that they are more attractive to the human eye. There are two classifications of gemstones — precious, such as diamonds or rubies, and semiprecious such as garnets and quartz.

They come in all shapes and sizes, each having its own set of unique characteristics. The base material the crystal emerges from determines how it will be formed. For example, crystals made from salt will form cube-like shapes, while snowflakes or ice crystals will form into lattices.

The process they go through when forming is referred to as crystallization. They naturally form in nature all around us. When the hot liquid (like magma) cools and then hardens, the liquid molecules start to bond together to create stability. As they do this, they create a uniform pattern that repeatedly repeats until they form a crystal. Other types of crystals are formed when water evaporates from a mixture. This is how salt crystals are created.

You can actually see this with your own eyes. If you want to try a little experiment, take a teaspoon of table salt and put it into regular tap water, and let it sit for 24 hours. When you check it again, you will see how the cube crystals have begun to form. These are created because as the water evaporates, the salt atoms are pulled closer together. As more water evaporates, the atoms will continue to pull together until they create a cluster. Eventually, you'll be able to see the cluster with the naked eye in the form of salt crystals.

You will notice that each crystal has its own distinctive shape, which develops based on the type of molecules and atoms at its base. It doesn't matter if the crystal is large or small, if it has the same base molecules and atoms, it will have the same shape.

Of course, not all crystals are formed so quickly, but they are all formed in the same way. Some like salt can be formed in a matter of days, but others, like those that are carbon-based, may take thousands of years to develop.

Natural crystals that have been formed within the earth's crust often take millions of years to develop. However, today many crystals are now being developed in laboratories. This is because a true crystal is extremely rare to find these days, but if you do have the privilege to own one, you will have in your possession an extremely powerful tool with the ability to do wonderful things.

Many people will sell you crystals, but they are not naturally formed. Natural crystals will always have some type of imperfection that can be spotted if you examine them closely. Those made in the laboratory will be perfect, absent of any flaws. Natural crystals can be dyed a different color or altered somehow, but a laboratory-made crystal can't be changed.

Another important difference is in the cost and the practicality of it. While a human-made crystal will have some level of energy, it will be far less than those that have been carefully made in the bowels of the earth for thousands of years. So, while they may be less expensive, you won't get the same results you get with natural crystals when you use them.

- **The Power Inside the Crystal**

You've probably already experienced the power and vibration in a room without even realizing it. It's that feeling you get when you're in a room full of happy people, everyone smiling, laughing, and enjoying themselves. Then without any explanation, another person enters the room, and the entire atmosphere changes. There seems to have been a sudden drain of energy, just by that person's presence.

This is called the Law of Vibration, and it shows that everything we see, touch, feel, hear, etc., is made up of energy, even our physical bodies. From the scientific perspective, there is little difference between you and the furniture in your room. Everything is the product of energy. This energy is constantly in motion, and the only difference is that all of it runs on different vibrations. Those that share the same energy and vibrations are considered the same.

As these energies vibrate, we develop thoughts, feelings, emotions and are spurred on to take different actions, which can affect the vibrations in some form. When we feel down and depressed, our vibrations are low and sluggish, but when we feel up and happy, our vibrations are faster, run at a higher frequency, and produce more energy.

We may not be aware that we emit these types of energies, but as we go about our day, we instinctively respond to those energies that are emanating all around us, and people are also responding to the energy we are putting out. So, if you start your day in a bad mood or on a low vibration, chances are the people around you will respond accordingly. You'll attract the same type of negative energy to you, and it will be difficult to move out of that low frequency if you are not aware of it.

The good news is that it doesn't have to be that way. You do have the ability to change it in much the same way as if you wanted to change what you were wearing that day. It all starts with changing the way you think. Once you change your thought process, you'll change your energy. This is the basics of the Law of Attraction. As a result of this change, you will be able to attract a different sort of people to you, those with a faster vibration than what you've normally been pulling in.

It is that energy that exists in all things that has the power to heal whatever it is that ails us. This is not something new or mystic but is at the core of many scientific discoveries. It is the kind of evidence that is used to back up physical theories for more than a century. Albert Einstein's theory of relativity is based on this very knowledge. It is the basis for nuclear power and will be the foundation of many new discoveries to come.

We might be inclined to believe that this energy only exists in living things, but we would be wrong. Even inanimate objects like crystals have their form of energy and vibrations, and it is when these two connect (humans and crystals), we begin to see amazing things happen.

Once we understand that all things vibrate, everything starts to become clear. While humans may not be able to sense or identify those vibrations automatically, they are there. The energy may present itself in three different ways through chakras, meridians, and auras in humans.

Chakras are the primary energy centers in every human body. Each person has seven different chakras that can be found in specific areas. It can be associated with a color and a number of other qualities.

- The first chakra is found at the base of the tailbone
- The second chakra or the sacral is found near the belly button
- The third chakra or the solar plexus sits at the base of the sternum
- The fourth chakra, the heart, sits right in the center of the chest
- The fifth chakra or the throat is found right above the Adam's apple
- The sixth chakra or the third eye sits directly in the center of the forehead
- And the seventh chakra or the crown can be found at the very top of the head

If you could visualize these chakras, you could draw a line directly from the first chakra at the base of the tailbone and draw it in a straight line all the way up through all of the other six, ending at the seventh chakra at the crown of the head.

Meridians are the paths of energy that are running through the body. Auras are the energy fields that are surrounding the body. These auras help us to identify energy in ourselves and in others. They work a little like special cameras for us.

Similar to human bodies, crystals also have their own vibrations and auras, and when the two forms of energy connect, crystal energy can have some sort of effect on our vibrations. They can help modify or adjust our energy and, as a result, bring about a certain element of healing. In other words, they can change how our energy vibrates.

Now that people recognize this internal energy and its effects on the human body, more people are exploring ways to tap into it. Besides through crystals, you might find other treatments once scoffed at becoming increasingly popular. Reflexology and Reiki are just two examples. In the following pages, we're going to show you several ways to use crystals to change your energy and vibrations.

- **Benefits of Using Crystals**

There are many different ways you can benefit from using crystals. Many have found that they help them mentally, emotionally, spiritually, and physically. Some have found practical use when they are used in conjunction with traditional Western-style medicine. If they are having a physical problem, they have found that using the crystals will lessen the discomfort they may be feeling or help to relieve the suffering altogether. But aside from easing physical ailments, there are other ways that crystals can be used to your benefit.

- They help you connect to your inner consciousness. They can help you to focus on that inner voice that is constantly running in your head.
- They can assist you psychologically so you can take more positive action in redirecting your life.
- They can clear away any emotional blockages that are getting in your way.
- They help clear away negative energy and thought patterns.

- And they can help you to tap into your more creative side.

We can understand how this is done by understanding the physics of human beings. While we are all made up of vibrating energy, our vibrations are not constant. When we are happy, our vibrations are usually much faster than when we are depressed. Our vibrations change from one day to the next and even from one situation to another. We're kind of all over the place. When we get close to someone with low vibration, our vibration usually comes down too. The same is true when we are in the same vicinity as those with a high vibration. We feel good, and we pick up on their emotions.

With crystals, it's different. These stones do not have emotions and feelings in the same sense that humans do. Therefore, their vibrations are always constant. They never change, and so they can provide us with a stabilizing effect that is hard for us to achieve on our own.

There are no set rules for how to use crystals. Some people benefit from their energy just by holding them in their hands.

Others will keep them close by, in their office, pockets, handbags, etc. Others sleep with them under their pillow, or they lie down and place them directly on one of their chakras.

While there are no specific guidelines for tapping into the crystal energy, you have to have your mind in the right place to gain the most benefit. But when the world is crowding in on you from all sides, it can be difficult to channel your mind in the right direction. Many who use crystals recommend meditation to help you. This is not something that can be done once in a while. To get the best results, one needs to make a daily practice of meditation for at least 10 to 20 minutes. It will help you to focus long enough to decide on the direction you want to go and what steps you want to take.

This can be a challenge initially, but those who make a habit of it, usually find that in time, they can learn to push out all of their worries and stresses and eventually tap into that inner voice in their head. One of the easiest forms of meditation today is practicing mindfulness. It doesn't require any position to take, nor do you have to worry about chanting any expressions or performing any rituals. You simply start to observe your thoughts as a neutral person through mindfulness, looking at them without judgment.

By doing this, you separate yourself from your thoughts, and eventually, you will learn to think more clearly. In time, you will feel as though you are a completely separate entity from your thoughts. Then you will be able to connect to your internal energy and channel crystal energy in the right direction.

Other forms of meditation you can adopt are guided imagery, mantra chanting, repetitive movement, and affirmations. Find the type of meditation that works best for you, and before long, you'll be able to tap into your energy field and gain the most benefits out of crystal energy.

Chapter 9.   Choosing Your Crystal

There are many different ways to choose crystals. We've already discussed that the crystals are the ones choosing your partnership, but it is still your responsibility to know when they are calling to you.

In order to choose correctly, you need to be very familiar with the condition you are trying to heal. Knowing your intention will help steer you in the right direction and allow the crystal to pick up on your vibes.

You can also choose your crystals by the way they appear to you. Crystals usually first draw people in because of their intrinsic natural beauty and striking colors. After this initial pull, you begin to notice the other features of a true crystal.

Sometimes crystals find their way to you through no act of your own. You may receive one as a gift, or you may discover one someplace near your home.

However,the way the crystal comes into your possession, follow your intuition. It is the best way to know for sure if the crystal is the right fit for your purposes. You may not realize it, but you are already gifted with the natural instinct to make this choice.

When you are drawn to a particular crystal, allow it to pull you in. Pick it up and hold it in the palm of your hand. Close your eyes and focus all of your energy on feeling the vibration and allow it to connect with your own inner vibrations. As you hold it, don't be surprised if you start to see images in your mind's eye. You may see a splash of color if you are strongly connected to it. If the crystal is not the right crystal for you, you will know it. You'll have a strong sense that something is not adding up, or you won't be able to connect with its vibrations.

There is a unique kind of mystery that surrounds the crystals that you have chosen. We recognize their energy but often do not understand it fully. It is said that crystals will only remain with you as long as you need their energy. Many people usually report that their crystals have suddenly disappeared after they have fulfilled their purpose. It is like they have returned back to the earth from where they have come. So don't be surprised to find your crystal missing after you've used it for a while. This is a good sign that you've healed and your purpose is fulfilled or that you now have a new purpose that another crystal may be better suited for.

Where to Buy Crystals

There are three ways to buy your crystals. Many people choose to buy them through online sites as they can be much cheaper than walking into a brick and mortar shop to purchase some rare form brought in from some distant region of the world.

However, buying online has its own drawbacks. One of the most important keys to choosing the right crystal is making a physical connection with it. Buying them online prevents you from doing this. In addition, there is no way you can determine the true authenticity of a stone without having the chance to examine it carefully.

This does not mean that all online dealers are deceptive. There are many dealers that produce crystals of a very high quality from online shops, and there are many individuals who are extremely intuitive and can choose a perfect crystal match just from looking at an image on their computer screen. In time, you will gain that kind of skill and talent, but for purchasing your first crystal, it is probably best to take a more tactile approach to select one that will work well for you.

Another way to purchase crystals is to visit events and shows. In fact, this is an excellent way to find unique crystals that have unusual shapes and patterns. When buying these types of crystals, keep in mind that you will be purchasing something that may have been handled by hundreds or even thousands of people before it finds its way to you. This can affect the kind of energy they emit so you may need to spend a little more time connecting with it before you make a decision.

Finally, you can purchase them through a brick and mortar shop. There are many specialty shops that deliver high-quality crystals on a more personal level. These are probably the best option for the beginner as the owners or workers in these shops have specialized knowledge that can help to guide you in making the right choice. They also allow you to closely inspect the stones and spend more time with it, so you can be sure that you're choosing the best one for you.

Choosing Crystal Shapes

You also want to pay close attention to the shape of the crystal you choose. While the healing properties within the crystal will remain constant regardless of the shape, the experience you have when connecting with it may differ because of it. There are many facets of crystal shapes you should be aware of that will help you to decide exactly which shape will work best for your needs.

The Point: Crystal points are those crystals that have intense energy and can channel or amplify it in many ways. You can use a crystal point to focus the energy inward when the point is facing you or outward by focusing it away. Points are one of the best starter crystals because their energy can be easily harnessed and directed to where you want it to go.

The Cube: Crystal cubes are often used when working with the root chakra. It is an excellent grounding stone that can bring in a powerful sense of calm to your environment. Cubes can also help you to create a protective grid surrounding your environment by placing one in each corner of your space.

The Pyramid: The pyramid is considered to be one of the sacred shapes used throughout many ancient civilizations. When you want to send out a concentrated beam of energy into the universe or make your intentions manifest, you would use the crystal pyramid by setting it on top of the paper you have written them on.

The Heart: The heart-shaped crystal is used as a reminder that you need to continue to use the healing properties and keep them close. People work with them as a form of spiritual nourishment that will help them to always give and accept energy sent out to them.

The Harmonizer: These cylinder-shaped crystals help you with meditation and make it easier for you to enter a more spiritually stimulated space. They also help with giving you a better sense of mental and physical balance.

The Cluster: Crystal clusters are some of the most beautiful creations found in nature. A cluster occurs only when you have many points that develop within the same matrix. Clusters generally vibrate at higher energy so having one in your sacred space will keep your energy levels high, so you have more power to work with.

Tumbled Stones: These stones can be used in a variety of ways. Those that are small with smooth surfaces can be carried in your pocket or purse. They are perfect pieces to make into jewelry and they are ideal of use in a crystal grid. They also make great starter stones because they are easy to use and draw energy from.

What to Look For

Knowing exactly what to look for in a crystal is extremely important as it is the one decision that will start you on your journey to balancing your energy and healing yourself. When it comes to buying these little gems, you want to be absolutely sure that you're getting the kind of quality you need. If you are intuitive enough to pick out a quality piece of crystal, you've saved yourself from a whole lot of headaches.

You can also look at the color of the crystal. There is no doubt that each color has its own healing properties. You can refer to a crystal directory for a detailed list of each color and their healing properties. These have a color and an image of each crystal categorized by its healing properties. However, below is a list of the most common colors and what they can do.

Black: Power, protection, and mystery. Black obsidian, black tourmaline, hematite, jet, and onyx are the most common black crystals used.

Blue: Tranquility and emotional healing. Angelite, aquamarine, apatite, blue lace agate, azurite, blue chalcedony, celestine, and chrysocolla.

Brown: Absorb negative energy and harness the healing powers of the earth. Smoky quartz, brown jasper, bronzite, tiger's eye, and petrified wood.

Yellow/Gold: From the color of the sun, these stones give optimism and joy. Amber, citrine, golden topaz, yellow tiger's eye, pyrite, and yellow jasper.

Green: Activates the heart chakra and provides an emotional balance. Brings good fortune and prosperity. Aventurine, emerald, green fluorite, jade, and malachite.

Orange: Arouse passion in the spirit. Captures the spirit and energy from the sun. aragonite, calcite, copper, carnelian, and sunstone.

Pink: Love and compassion, heart energizers, and opens up the heart. Pink tourmaline, pink sapphire, rose quartz, and lepidolite.

Grey: Reflects the moonlight and the expanse of the universe. Provides protective shield. Hematite and moonstone.

Purple: Gives enlightenment and intuition. They keep emotions balanced and provide relaxing and soothing vibes. They can also amplify the energy, especially when used with the heart chakra. Amethyst and charoite.

Red: Infuses passion and has a grounding energy that supports the root chakra. Garnet, ruby, and red tiger's eye.

White: Represents purity and transformation. Excellent healing tools when used with other healing grids. Clear quartz and selenite.

You can also look for stones based on the chakra you want to heal.

Crown Chakra: Selenite and clear quartz

The Third Eye: Lapis lazuli, sodalite, and fluorite

The Throat Chakra: Aquamarine, angelite, blue apatite, sodalite

The Heart Chakra: Aventurine and rhodonite

Solar Plexus Chakra: Pyrite, rutilated quartz, citrine, and yellow jasper

Sacral Chakra: Carnelian, orange calcite, tiger's eye, and sunstone.

Root Chakra: Black onyx, red garnet, red jasper, hematite, and smoky quartz.

There are many ways to look for the right crystal for you. If you're still not sure, don't be shy about asking the shopkeeper to assist you. They work with these stones every day and have a highly trained intuitiveness that helps them match you with the right crystal.

What to Avoid

Buying crystals can be a little scary at first. You walk into a nice little shop and you may see hundreds of crystals on display. Unlike heading into your local supermarket where all produce is placed together and the deli counter has all the cuts you want, crystal shop owners do not have such a regimented way to display their wares. It is left entirely up to the individual owners so what may work for you in one shop may not be the same at the next shop.

This makes it hard to walk into the store and quickly find exactly what you're looking for. So don't hesitate to browse and ask questions. Still, while crystal healing is a noble occupation, it doesn't mean that all the shop owners are equally as noble. There are some major pitfalls you will want to be aware of.

Natural or Manmade: Now that modern science has been able to imitate the creation of a crystal in the laboratory, synthetic crystals should cost far less than natural ones. Examine the crystal closely looking for flaws. If it seems too perfect with no flaws, it's a good chance it is manmade and it won't bring you the same kind of power that comes from those crystals that have been shaped by millions of years in the earth.

Labels: You also want to keep a close eye out for stones with a trademark name or that comes with an excessively high price tag. Any name that is trademarked may be the same quality as one that is not, but they will cost a great deal more.

Check for Alternations: Some crystals may have been altered from their natural state. This may also alter the effectiveness of the crystal. Some shop owners may change the appearance of a crystal so that it looks more like another crystal. They may dye it, heat it, or coat it so that it appears to be another stone with completely different properties.

There are many ways you can "fake" a crystal. It may have started out as a partially real crystal but when you coat the exterior or combine it with a synthetic, like what is often done with opals and turquoise, you may find yourself buying mostly glass. Rubies are another crystal that is often altered in some way.

To determine if it's a fake, you can ask the seller, but if it is, he's not likely going to tell you. However, there are a few other steps you can take to be sure.

Check the base for any signs of mounting, glue, or paint.

Look for uneven coloring or shades not normally found in nature.

Look into the glass for signs of air bubbles

Look for flaws. All naturally occurring crystals have flaws. If it looks too perfect, chances are, it is.

While there may be many crystals that can be altered in some form, you should watch some common crystals. Since finding authentic turquoise is rare, it can be quite expensive. Sellers will usually make a synthetic stone that is made from dyed resin or ceramic. They may also substitute it with how lite, which has veins that are very similar to turquoise veins. You can identify fake turquoise quite easily. First, its blue color will appear unnatural, and there will be brown lines running through it.

Another crystal to be cautious of is citrine. Most of what you will see in a crystal shop is not authentic citrine, but amethyst has been heat-treated until it turns to the desired yellow color. The heat will actually change the stone's properties, so it is always important to get some sort of authentication before you make a purchase.

Chapter 10. Crystals And Chakras

As mentioned above, there are seven major chakras in your body and each of these chakras is a center for energy. Each chakra is associated with a major organ and provides the concerned organ with the necessary energy for its optimal functioning. Apart from this, chakras are also associated with specific aspects of behavior, as well as development. Your state of health and balance are determined through the energy that flows in these chakras. It is quintessential that your chakras are in balance to ensure your mental, physical, spiritual, and emotional well-being. In this section, you will learn about the different chakras and their healing properties.

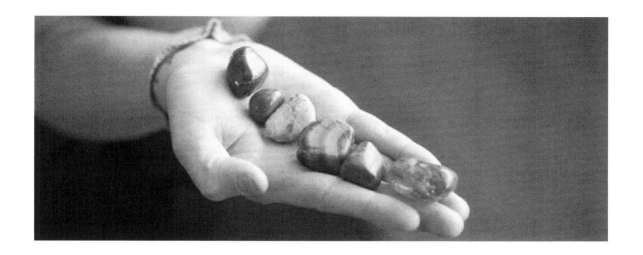

First chakra

The first chakra is known as the root chakra. The root chakra is located at the base of your spine right behind the pubis and is associated with vitality. This chakra is also connected to the adrenaline gland. The root chakra is believed to be the basis of life as well as being the energy flowing in the human body. This chakra establishes the balance of the flow of inward energy and outward vibrancy. It also helps regulate the mechanisms that are keeping you alive. Your survival instinct is determined by the root chakra. So, if there is any blockage in this chakra, you will feel tired quite easily. The color associated with the root chakra is red. If you want to clear any energy blockage in this chakra, then the crystals you can use are coral, garnet, ruby, jasper, or other red crystals. The element associated with the root chakra is worth. So, by keeping your body close to the earth, you can help balance this chakra. It is also symbolized by a square. When this chakra is functioning like it's supposed to, it ensures that your adrenaline glands are functioning well.

The second chakra

The second chakra is also known as the sacral chakra. This chakra is situated below the navel, and it is responsible for controlling one's sexual urges. It is believed that the energy generated by this chakra is an integral point for all the relationships you have in life. It essentially controls your feelings in your relationships. A block in the energy of this chakra can create sexual troubles. The color associated with this chakra is orange, and the shape related to it is an upturned crescent. Various stones or crystals that are orange in color like orange carnelian, moonstone, or orange calcite, can be used for balancing this chakra. If you want to heal this chakra, you must place the respective stones as close to your navel. Water is the element associated with this chakra. There are two opposing features associated with water, and they are servility and stability. If you want to be centered and grounded, then there needs to be a balance between these polarities. Once you attain this, the energies in your body can start flowing freely.

The third chakra

The third chakra is also known as the solar plexus chakra. As its name suggests, it is located right above your navel and close to your solar plexus. The solar plexus is believed to be the anatomical center of your body and the center of your mental consciousness. It regulates focus and willpower. This chakra tends to give an individual a sense of completion and contentment. Two polarities exist in your mind and they are definite in this and the willingness to be opened. The solar plexus chakra helps maintain this balance. The color associated with this chakra is yellow and its symbol is that of an inverted triangle. Various stones like topaz, calcite, and malachite can be used to remove any blocks in this chakra and maintain its balance. The element associated with this chakra is fire.

The fourth chakra

The fourth chakra is also known as the heart chakra. As its name suggests, it is located at the center of your chest, close to your heart. This chakra is essentially the meeting point of the spiritual realm to your reality. It is a center for unconditional love for others as well as for yourself. It is believed to be a bridge between the higher and the lower energies that exist in your body. It also helps in understanding the difference between discernment and inclusiveness. The heart chakra can help you realize that you must accept yourself and others without any judgment or fear. Only when the energies of this chakra are balanced will you be able to welcome love into your life. This love doesn't necessarily have to be from others, but it can also be self-love. The color associated with the heart chakra is green and it is symbolized by two intertwined triangles, which are pointing in opposite directions. The different stones that can be used to remove any blocks in this chakra and heal it are emerald, jade, and moss agate.

The fifth chakra

All the chakras after the fourth chakra tend to be inclined towards your spiritual and emotional well-being. The fifth chakra is referred to as the throat chakra and is located near your throat. This chakra is responsible for your speech, ability to communicate, and self-expression. The fifth chakra is also associated with the inner voice that you keep hearing in your head. The different organs associated with this chakra are the upper part of the lungs, the digestive tract, thyroid gland, and throat. If there is an energy blockage in this chakra, it can cause any of these organs. Any difficulty in communicating, fear, doubt, or even habitual lying are all associated with imbalances in the throat chakra. The color associated with this chakra is light blue and it is symbolized by a circle presented within an inverted triangle. The stones you can use to balance the energy in this chakra are aquamarine, turquoise, and amazonite. The element that is associated with this chakra is ether.

The sixth chakra

The sixth chakra is also known as the third-eye chakra. This chakra is located right between the eyebrows, in the middle of the forehead. This chakra helps in striking a balance between radiant light and luminous light. The third eye chakra is closely related to your intuition. Your intuition is triggered only when there exists both lights as well as dark within you. It is believed that when there is a void of darkness, a person will be able to find the light. This chakra is closely associated with feelings of compassion and forgiveness. If there is a block in the energy in this chakra, it often causes confusion and indecisiveness. Your eyes, pituitary gland, and the lower part of your brain are all related to this chakra. So, any troubles in this chakra can cause migraines. The color associated with this chakra is indigo, and the stones related to it are fluorites, azurite, black obsidian, and amethyst.

The seventh chakra

The seventh and final chakra is also known as the crown chakra. As its name suggests, it is located at the crown of your head. This chakra is often representative of the highest level of enlightenment. Also, this is one of the most difficult chakras to unlock. It essentially is the center of a person's spirit. It brings together the energies of all the chakras and helps maintain peace. Since it is located at the top of your head, it is connected to the pineal gland. The color associated with this chakra is violet and it is symbolized by a lotus, which has over a thousand patterns within it. The stones related to this chakra are amethyst, clear quartz, diamond, and selenite. Apart from this, you can also use clear crystals or white stones to cleanse your aura.

Now that you're aware of the different chakras and the way crystals are associated with each of them, it will make it easier to select the right crystals.

Chapter 11.   30 Crystal to Know

Since the earliest times, recordings of healing with stones and crystals are found. Many different ways of the application were used, but all focused on the same goal – healing! The healing properties of stones and crystals are numerous, and there are too many to be named here. For the purpose of this book, some of the most popular healing stones will be used. It is always best to look for the stone that best fits your needs.

It is important to state that crystals or stones alone won't do anything to the body that the body doesn't want to be done. A perfect state of health is to maintain a perfect balance between spirit, soul, and body. As crystals and stones come from the earth and have similar minerals as what we are made of, it helps balance our bodies' energysoftly and gently. Healing with stones should never be a substitute for healing in a professional manner.

Health and Healing

1. Amethyst:

Amethyst has a calming and soothing energy that helps the transmitting of neurons in the brain. It is associated with the Crown Chakra or Third Eye. As a protective stone, it naturally tranquilizes and helps to alleviate stress and anxiety. It helps the body to be rid of negative and harmful energy. It helps against insomnia. It also strengthens the immune system and helps to balance the hormones and endocrine system. With the beautiful tones of deep purple to lilac, it brings a sense of harmony and tranquility to any room, and it is very popular to have some Amethyst stones in your room.

2. Crystal Quartz:

This crystal is one of the most common stones found almost all over the world. It has an amazing ability to structure, store, transmit and control frequencies. That is why even the electronic world uses it. For healing purposes, crystal quartz properties work like a tuning fork bringing our bodies back to a healthier state. It projects all forms of energies known to us and therefore serves as an ideal unlocker of energy in our body. Crystal Quartz opens All Chakras but activates the Crown Chakra.

3. Herkimer Diamond:

Known as an attunement stone Herkimer helps you to attune with others and your environment. It is powerful in releasing pain as the energy starts to circulate in a very short time. It cleanses the body of toxins and is also known to correct cellular disorders. The Third Eye Chakra is the primary chakra it is related to, but it is also associated with the Crown Chakra. It is very effective in re-aligning energy. This potent balancing stone sets physical and spiritual energies in order. An elixir of this stone is perfect for a weakened body. Let the stone stand overnight in clear spring water and take it in the morning to feel rejuvenated.

4. Clear Quartz

This is the best crystal to use for healing. This has no negative effects whatsoever but needs to be cleansed before you use it. You will be able to clear different types of energies in your body – physical, mental, spiritual and emotional. You will be able to align all the energies in your body. This crystal can be cleaned easily. You will find it very easy to program the crystal to balance all the energies in your body. You will be able to create a great impression on your soul.

5. Onyx

This crystal helps in balancing the opposing forces of energy – the yin and the yang. You will be able to reduce any form of stress in your body when you use this crystal. You will also be able to exercise a good level of self–control and will be able to find happiness in the smallest things. Good fortune becomes your very good friend.

6. Opal

The opal crystal is a brilliant one since it works on improving all your attributes. You will be able to enhance your creativity and imagination. A student would love this crystal since he or she would be able to improve his memory that would prove beneficial for them during the examinations. It also helps in removing any inhibitions you may have!

7. Peridot

This crystal helps in inspiring you. It will strengthen you from within and will regenerate you! You will be able to obtain great levels of protection when you use this stone. Every bit of anger or jealousy you may have will be washed off when you sue this stone.

8. Amethyst

This crystal has the ability to convert all the negative energy in your body to positive energy. You will be able to access your subconscious when you use this crystal. You will be able to access your meditative state during the healing process. It is because of this that you can use this to heal your third eye chakra! The stone is extremely spiritual and helps you access the higher self. This crystal like the clear quartz is very good for spiritual healing. You will be able to transform and heal yourself.

9. Pyrite

This crystal helps in removing any form of negativity from your body. You will be able to purge your body of any pessimism. You will find yourself becoming optimistic and also trying to understand the greater aspects of life. You will be able to improve your memory and intellect.

10.   Rhodonite

This is a crystal that works best to improve your confidence and your self – esteem. You will find yourself with decreased levels of anxiety and will also be able to obtain a certain level of balance in your life. You will begin to look at the bigger picture and will be able to understand things at a greater length. This crystal helps you attain your true potential!

## 11.	Lapis Lazuli

This is a crystal that is used to cleanse your mind and purge it of all negative thoughts. You will also be able to calm your mind when you use this crystal. You will find yourself with a free flow of thought and will be able to protect yourself from making any hasty decisions. If you place this crystal near your third eye chakra, you will be able to open the mind that will make you more knowledgeable. You will also be able to widen your horizons. If you are a student, you will find that this crystal has helped you focus on your courses and has helped you attain undivided focus on a particular task at hand. This crystal works wonders when you use it at work too. The best part about this crystal is that it helps you remember all your dreams, hence the name dream–catcher.

12.   Tourmaline

This stone is called the protection stone since it creates a protective shield around your body and your mind to ward off any negativity. You will also be able to remove any amount of fear that you may feel. You will be able to enhance your inspiration and will also be able to learn on your own. Your confidence will be given a great boost!

13.   Hematite

This crystal is the perfect friend for your mind. This crystal works towards purging your mind from any negative thoughts. These thoughts are terrible for you since they bring you down mentally and emotionally. Your mind will begin to open itself up to learn more and will start observing the world around you more. The advantage of this crystal is that you will be able to remove any inhibitions you may have with respect to the different aspects of your life. If you use this crystal along with clear quartz, you will be able to regain the balance of your mind. Your blood will be cleansed too when you use this crystal.

14.   Moonstone

This is a crystal that women often use since it always keeps them calm during pregnancy and during the menstrual cycle. The energy is always balanced and so are the thoughts in the mind. It is because of this crystal that clairvoyants find their capabilities increasing and sharpening. You will also be able to balance certain areas in your body using this crystal. You will also be able to keep any negative emotions at bay.

15.   Pyrite

Students often use this crystal to help them perform well during any examination. Professionals also use this crystal when they are looking for different ways to improve their work ethic. When a person possesses this crystal, he will find a boost in his self – esteem. The properties of this crystal work best when it is worn on the body like an ornament.

16.   Smokey Quartz

This crystal is a wonder since it always finds a way to absorb any pain you may be feeling. It acts as the neutral wire in an electric cable and will help you remove any negative energy in your body through the process of grounding. The earth absorbs all the negative energy in your body. This process leaves you with a sense of security and will help remove any depression you may face.

17.   Rose Quartz

This crystal is one that depicts every aspect of love. You will find that this crystal works best with your heart chakra. You will be able to understand your heart better and will be able to understand all your feelings. You will also be able to increase your trust and faith in the people around you. You will be able to love yourself unconditionally which will help in introducing you to your inner self. You will also be able to remove any depression and grief. The love that you have for yourself will help you overcome any negative thoughts you may have about yourself. Any resentment that you feel towards the people around you will vanish when you use this crystal. The best combination of this crystal is amethyst.

18.   Agate

This is the strongest stone and it leaves you with a lot of courage. It strengthens your body and your mind. You will be able to perceive the environment around you in a better fashion. You will begin to be precise. The crystal also helps in grounding you and leaving you with immense energy. The best part about this crystal is that the energies in your body, both the yin and yang, will be balanced soon.

19.   Amazonite

This crystal is another delight! It helps in creating a balance between your physical body and the astral body. It also helps in aligning the energy in your body. The crystal helps in calming you down and also helps in enhancing your creativity by giving you the power of imagination.

## 20.	Aquamarine

This crystal has the power to provide you with emotional support and intellectual stability. It has the power to clear your mind and is often used by people when they are meditating. You will be able to express yourself easily and will be able to develop a certain level of tolerance towards the people around you. You will also be able to strengthen the image you have of yourself and remove any phobia you may have.

21.   Aventurine

This crystal is a wonder since it has the ability to balance all the opposing forces in your body. You will be able to find yourself thinking positively and will feel independent. You will begin to work on projects you had never thought you would opt for before. All your anxiety will be washed away if you use this crystal.

22.   Azurite

This is another crystal that can be used to cleanse the mind and the soul. You will be able to awaken your third eye and will be able to perceive numerous entities around you when you begin to use this crystal. You will find yourself beginning to change! The other advantage of using this crystal is that you will be able to find inspiration in the littlest of things thereby enhancing your creativity.

23.   Bloodstone

This is a stone that works wonders when it used in the healing processes. The crystal helps in revitalizing and rejuvenating the mind and the body. You will be able to keep yourself happy and calm throughout your life. You will find yourself wiser than ever before and will be able to sense your ultimate self or your inner soul very often. You will then be able to make the right decisions throughout your life.

24.   Turquoise:

This is a truth stone and master healer. As a communication stone, it helps public speaking but also verbalizing your own problems. On a physical level, it helps to release stress and is a regenerator. It is good for headaches and circulation. This helps in viral infections and lung problems. It is related to the Throat Chakra and it also helps to absorb nutrients and strengthen the immune system.

25. Carnelian:

This stone is an active stone that removes blocked energy. It is associated with the Sacral Chakra. Wearing it increases vitality and positive thinking. On the physical side, it helps with blood circulation and problems with the kidneys, bladder, spleen and liver. It is also known to help allergies related to pollen and neuralgia. As a creative stone, it augments a fighting spirit to reach and fulfill goals.

26.   Bloodstone:

As a grounding stone, Bloodstone is excellent in calming difficult situations. It releases blockages and is very helpful in emotional traumas. It is related to the Root Chakra and also cleanses the Lower Chakras. It is used to treat anaemia and blood-related illnesses. It can also be used to treat diabetes and post-surgical treatment.

27.   Lapis Lazuli:

It is a stone that acts as a protector against psychic attacks and brings inner-peace and self-knowledge. It relates to the Throat Chakra and Third Eye Chakra. It furthermore boosts the immune system and purifies the blood, and soothes areas of inflammation. It helps treat the respiratory system, especially the throat and thyroid.

28. Black Tourmaline:

This is a powerful protection stone against negative energy and also acts as a grounding stone. A very popular stone for metaphysical purposes. It absorbs negative electromagnetic energy and helps the body to restore the electric field. It is related to the Root Chakra. It is a purifying stone and very helpful to have in all the areas of your home or office.

29. Fluorite:

This stone is associated with the Heart, Throat and Third Eye Chakras. It cleanses and absorbs negative energy. It helps with concentration and brings balance to us. It is a regenerating stone that helps with the restructuring of cells and DNA and strengthens the respiratory tract. It is very good to use when you have shingles or other nerve-related diseases as it eases the pain going with it.

30.   Jade:

As a balancing stone, it offers wealth, health, and love. It opens the Heart Chakra and brings inner peace. It is very soothing for the nerves and is relaxing and calming overall. It furthermore brings healing energy into the gallbladder, liver, bladder, and kidneys. It is a regenerator stone too. Throughout centuries, Jade is used to helping with depression. Wearing it in the form of a bracelet is very soothing and brings a lovely calmness.

Chapter 12.   Basic Meditation

Meditation is strongly related to mystical experiences and Kundalini syndromes. According to a study, it is more effective than yoga and prayer in creating Kundalini syndromes. This may be because meditation involves an inner focus, which is not always involved in yoga or prayer. After all, meditation goes beyond a particular religious belief or practice, and it is something that is shared by varying cultures throughout history.

Because regular meditators experience Kundalini more often, it may mean that the meditations cause it or because dedicated meditators are predisposed for Kundalini experiences. No matter what the case may be, you will benefit if you regularly meditate. Not only will you train your mind to make it more capable of directing and withstanding energy, you will also receive perks like improved moods, self-control and overall health.

Mystical traditions assert that meditating upon a deity, a guru, a holy man/woman or a sacred concept will make you acquire their energetic qualities. This can mean gazing at a picture of them, chanting their name or mantra, imagining them, or emotionally connecting to them. There are certain gurus who are said to convey Shaktipat to their disciples by letting them connect to their energy via meditation.

Transcendental Meditation may activate the Kundalini – some of those who practice TM have experienced the Kundalini syndrome. This involves meditation with a mantra that may be given by the guru. An often-used mantra is "ongnamo guru dev namo" which is translated to "I bow to the divine within." This connects your energy to a line of enlightened masters, ensuring that the wisdom you receive is reliable and the energy controlled.

Meditation and Multiple Practices

Based on research on meditators and Kundalini experiencers, meditation and multiple transpersonal practices increase the chances of Kundalini awakening.

It was discovered that the total amount of practice is more important than the frequency, pattern, and social conditions of practicing (de Castro, 2015). This means that it's good if you meditate a lot of times so the effect will accumulate.

- **Prayer**

Prayer leads to mystical experiences when there are positive emotions like adoration and gratitude. When prayer involves requests or confession of sins or done out of obligation, mystical experiences occur less frequently. When praying, include in your intention that you want to be closer to God or to your idea of the Divine. You may ask that this happen specifically via Kundalini awakening, but sometimes it may occur in another form. Catholics or Christians may experience the Holy Spirit's descent – it is similar to the Kundalini but in a form that their belief systems are already predisposed to accept.

- **Yoga**

There are many kinds of yoga; some deal specifically with Kundalini activation. Regardless of whether yoga is done for Kundalini or not, Kundalini will more likely be awakened if yoga is practiced contemplatively. In contrast, if yoga is done mechanically and treated only as a means to attain fitness, Kundalini will remain dormant.

Yoga generally deals with physical exercises (asanas and mudras), chanting (mantras), breath control (pranayama), meditation, concentration, and visualization.

Some forms of yoga that deal with Kundalini are the following:

- Kundalini yoga/Laya yoga: Kundalini yoga incorporates Hatha yoga, Kriya yoga, visualization and meditation.

- Hatha yoga: Particular Hatha yoga practices are said to raise Kundalini such as mula bandha, jalandhara bandha, kechari mudra, kumbhaka, and mula bandha.

- Kriya yoga: Kriya yoga involves self-study, self-discipline, and devotions.

- Sahaja yoga: Sahaja yoga teaches Kundalini activation methods to enable a person to achieve self-realization.

Yoga is considered as a structured path. These Kundalini-based Yoga forms have specific techniques for activating, maintaining, and making use of Kundalini for different purposes. You can learn Yoga on your own but to be sure you carry out the techniques properly, it's best to attend a class.

Yoga improves the interconnections between the mind and body, making you more capable of directing subtle energies at will. It will make you aware of your limitations so you can surpass them. Although the postures and movements may be difficult, they will make you familiar with how your physical, mental, and energy bodies work, and eventually, you will learn how to control them so they serve you better.

Kriya Yoga

Kriya Yoga is one form of yoga that is said to be a safer alternative to forcing the Kundalini upwards. According to ParamhansaYogananda – a yoga master from India that brought Kundalini knowledge to the West – Kriya Yoga is a technique that combines the right attitude and purity of heart with life force stimulation so that problems are avoided.

Kriyas are "activities" and can be linked to the spontaneous movements that tend to occur upon the awakening of the Shakti. The kriyas help remove the blocks that stand in the way of the kundalini as it traverses the central channel and spine. They are triggered by the energy's interaction with the blockages.

There is a belief that the higher chakras are positive magnets that pull the consciousness upwards towards the divine, while the chakra at the spine's base pulls it downwards towards ignorance, selfishness, and materialism. In this belief system, the Kundalini is the thrust of consciousness that is related to matter, and it causes the restlessness of the mind during meditation.

The goal of guiding the Kundalini upwards is to pull it away from its negative position and unite it with the positive magnet at the top of the head. The problem is, many practices just aim to shake this energy loose. However, this energy is quite dangerous, and overstimulating it causes extreme heat that may damage the person's nervous system and cause psychological disturbances.

Kriya Yoga is safer and easier than other practices, and it can also pave the way towards spiritual enlightenment. Because it's a holistic discipline, it can improve your physical and psychological well-being. Basically, it involves the cleansing of the energy channels so that energies can move more freely in the body.

These are some of the things under Kriya Yoga that can help with awakening the energy:

- Have love for the divine. This means going beyond simply practicing religious rituals just because you are taught to do them, but having a genuine desire to commune and unite with your God.

- See everything and everyone as manifestations of the Divine. The truth is, the Universe is a part of the one who created it, so you must have respect for creation as well.

- Have a positive attitude. Although life will inevitably make you feel negative at times, do your best not to get stuck in negativity. Activating Kundalini means you have to keep your energy channels clear and your frequency high.

- Do things that cause spiritual expansion. Activities that cause upliftment to yourself and others have benefits to your spiritual condition. This could be anything such as learning a productive skill, being generous to others, helping out with a cause, etc.

- Acknowledge your higher nature. All people have lower and higher natures but not all of them live as spiritual beings. The more that you are conscious of your spiritual aspect, the better your chances are of progressing spiritually.

- Develop greater awareness. Prevent yourself from going deeper into unconsciousness by indulging in things that dull your mind. Be more mindful. Participate in meaningful and productive endeavors. Try not to do things that you know are nonsensical or detrimental to you or others.

- Chanting with a devotional attitude may raise your Kundalini. Take note that inciting mantras half-heartedly may be useless.

- Be energetic. Find things to do that give you energy. Dedicate yourself to things you are passionate about. These have effects to your subtle energies as well.

- Interestingly, waking the stored Kundalini energy can be done not only by stirring it and forcing it to shoot up from below, but it can also be coaxed upward by drawing it from above. To do this, you must make your higher chakras magnetic.

- Meditating upon saints, mystics, deities, and other spiritual personas will help you with this. By calling upon them, they may help you awaken your spirituality.

Basically, the things mentioned above can help you be in touch with your spiritual nature whether you practice Kriya yoga or not. If you want to follow the path of Kriya yoga, here's a simplified version of how to do it:

Procedure

Develop and keep a good posture. Be mindful that your spine is straight for as often as you can. This will be beneficial not only to your physical health and energy level but also to your Kundalini in its ascent.

Be physically active. Kriya Yoga is all about balance, so you have to balance meditation with physical exercise. Moving your body will help with removing unclean and used energy. Aerobic exercises will invigorate you and directly help move the Kundalini, but you may also do mild exercises such as simple stretches, head rolls, and the like.

Sit on a chair with your feet flat or on the floor in the crossed leg or lotus position. Keep your spine straight, and your head parallel to the ground. Close your eyes and remove all distractions and preoccupations from your mind.

Focus entirely on your breath. The breath is prana, so you must be sensitive to your respirations to work with subtle energy. Using your mind, you will direct it to bring up the Kundalini upwards through the seven chakras that line your spine.

Feel your breath stirring in the base of your spine. You may feel it becoming warmer when you do so. This is the energy becoming activated. Just accept it and bring it upwards with each breath. Be sensitive to it. Notice what it's doing. Do not force it to move but gently coax it. It will untangle coils and burn impediments on its own.

Continue bringing your breath up until you feel energy running along your spine. When you feel that the energy has reached the topmost chakra, bring your breath down one chakra at a time until you reach the heart.

Inhale from the bottom of your spine again to bring up the energy to the crown. As you exhale, bring the energy down and let it go out of your heart. This is a more balanced form of awakening; try this if you're overwhelmed by raising Kundalini from the bottom up.

Purification

Hindu tradition requires the cleansing and strengthening of the body to prepare it for the passage of Kundalini. Fasting is sometimes prescribed - this may mean not eating for a certain number of days or not eating particular kinds of food like red meat. Activities that entertain the senses are likewise prohibited from refreshing the mind and making it concentrate on spirituality.

Traditionally, kundalini awakening is done in a learning setting. There are still gurus who go handpick worthy students to impart teachings that they don't share with anybody else. Nowadays, anyone who wants to learn may go to a guru or join a workshop.

Kundalini Spiritual Awakening

Kundalini awakenings happen differently for everyone. For some, they are slow and come in persistently but over time. It can be extremely quick for others, almost like an explosion of energy in the gut area. Either way, Kundalini awakenings can be quite intense for anyone who experiences them.

Here are some of the symptoms you can expect to experience during your awakening.

Remember, not everyone will experience all of the same symptoms. Furthermore, you may experience some that have not been listed here. That is okay, too. The goal is to be one with the process and welcome anything that comes your way.

Everything Seems to Fall Apart

One of the first things many people experience in the face of their awakening is feelings of nervousness. As you awaken, it may feel like everything is falling apart. This is because the world as you have come to know it is being perceived through the eyes of someone who has Kundalini that is still dormant. As a result, you may feel like everything as you know it falls away.

Many people who awaken will experience massive life changes as a result of this falling apart. Several of the aspects of their lives that are not aligned with their awakened energies will begin to drift away as they make room for new, aligned experiences in their lives. Although this is generally all for the best in the long run, you can feel intense bouts of chaos and stress in the midst of everything falling apart. Sometimes, people will even block their awakening to lessen the chaos and prevent the stress from increasing.

Everything that has been used as a crutch to support your unhealed self will begin to render itself as useless as you realize that they are no longer supporting you. This can, of course, be scary. Many call this "leaving their comfort zone" because they are venturing beyond the system they have carefully built around themselves to bring some peace and comfort into their lives. However, they will virtually always end up finding a more pure and true sense of comfort later in their lives when they enter a later phase of their awakening.

Physical Symptoms

Many individuals that undergo awakening experience physical symptoms as a part of the process. These symptoms are generally very random and are not linked to any health issues carried by the individual. Of course, if you do experience any ongoing physical symptoms that are particularly alarming, you should always contact your physician to rule out anything serious. However, realize that if nothing comes back and you remain "undiagnosed," it is likely that these are symptoms of your awakening.

Some of the physical symptoms people experience include anything from shaking to visual disturbances. Some will also struggle to relax due to the major rushes of energy that course through their bodies. Others still may even experience near-death experiences that either contributes to the awakening or result from the awakening. Remember, whatever symptoms you experience, if you are at all concerned, you should certainly contact a physician. Even though they may be spiritual awakening symptoms, it is always important to take proper precautionary methods and look after your physical body.

Many people will experience physical symptoms because their physical body is simply unable to handle such a rush of energy. As the awakening continues, these symptoms should subside. The body will grow more accustomed to the incoming energies and will likely find it significantly easier to handle. Feeling physical symptoms may encourage you to deny your awakening, but as long as you are truly healthy, enduring them can lead to powerful results. If you are particularly concerned, you can always work alongside a Kundalini master to receive support and guidance on managing these symptoms and potentially slowing them down to make them more manageable as you endure your awakening. In general, your physical, emotional, and energetic symptoms should last only about 20 minutes at a time.

Emotional Symptoms

Emotional symptoms are extremely common in Kundalini awakenings. In fact, they are felt by virtually everyone who experiences their awakening. Emotional symptoms vary, but early on the most common symptoms include anxiety, despair, and depression. The emotions can also range in the opposite direction, bringing intense feelings of delight, joy, and an overwhelming sense of peace to the individual.

These emotional fluctuations are directly the result of the changing energy within your body. At first, they may be intense and overwhelming. You may feel as though you are encountering and enduring many mood swings, making it challenging to deal with. The best thing that you can do is allow yourself to embody the emotions and feel through them. Refrain from blocking them or resisting them, as this can result in you directly resisting your awakening.

Energetic Symptoms

The primary energetic symptoms experienced by individuals experiencing a Kundalini awakening are massive influxes of energies at seemingly random times. These energies can become quite powerful, resulting in people randomly feeling extremely energized and even restless. These energy symptoms are inevitable, as spiritual awakenings do exist in the non-physical life-force energy of Kundalini. You may experience many symptoms as a result. Virtually all emotional and physical symptoms stem from the energetic symptoms of your awakening.

One interesting aspect of energetic symptoms is that many will go unnoticed. Because these are less tangible than physical and emotional symptoms, many things will go on in the background to contribute to your overall shift. The best thing you can do to manage energetic symptoms is to find peace, allow them to flow, and work through anything that they bring your way, either physically or energetically. The more you allow them to move through, the better it will become for you.

Chapter 13.   Kriya Yoga - Prana and Apana

Prana and Apana are the body's two dominant currents. The two distinct roles of the life force, such as prana and Apana, are discussed in this Gita verse. Since there is an arm wrestling on a macrocosmic scale that represents the Spirit's projecting desire to Create and His opposite attractive desire to get the many back to the One, it often happens at a microcosmic level in the human body. The relation between prana and Apana is an example of this positive-negative duality.

In the body, there are two major currents. The first is the Apana present, which runs from the point between the brows to the coccyx. This descending flow is transmitted to the sensory and motor nerves through the coccygeal core, holding man's consciousness illusorily connected to the body. The restless Apana current drives man toward sensory experiences.

Prana, which runs from the coccyx to the point between the eyebrows, is the other major current. This life current is peaceful in nature; it internally withdraws the devotee's focus during sleep and waking hours, and it unites the soul with the Spirit in the

Christ Centre in the brain during meditation. As a result, the falling current (Apana) and the ascending current (Apana) wield opposing forces (prana). The tug of war between these two currents to bind or free the soul pushes human consciousness up and down. The vital current flowing out of the brain and backbone towards cells, tissues, and nerves becomes attached and entangled in matter. It is used, like electricity, through the body's motor movements (voluntary and involuntary) and mental activity. As life in cells, tissues, and nerves begin to end because of this notoriety and sense-perceptual activity - especially through excessive, non-harmonious, unbalanced actions - prana works to recharge them and keep them vital. However, in consuming vital energy, they dispose of junk products, "decay." One of these products is carbon dioxide excreted by cells in the venous system; the immediate purifying prana action becomes necessary to remove the accumulation of this "decay"; otherwise, death could soon occur. The physiology of this exchange is breathing.

Breath: the rope that binds the soul to the body

The opposite attraction of the currents of prana and Apana in the spine was born to the breath's inspirations and expirations. When the current of prana rises, it pushes the vital oxygen-laden breath into the lungs. Prana quickly distills the necessary amount of life force from the electronic and vitatronic composition of the oxygen atoms. (It takes more time for prana to distill life force from coarse liquids and solid foods in the stomach.)

This refined energy is sent by the current of prana to all the body cells; without thus a replacement of pure vital energy, the cells would be devoid of energy to perform their many physiological functions; die. Lifeforce distilled from oxygen also helps to strengthen the life force centers in the spine and the point between the eyebrows and the main reservoir of vital energy in the brain. The blood carries the oxygen surplus that has been inspired through the body, where it is used by the five vital pranas in various physiological processes.

As noted, the activity of the body produces decay and the consequent production of carbon dioxide waste. This waste is excreted by the cells through the Apana current or eliminated and is transported through the blood to the lungs. Then the downward Apana current in the spine causes exhalation and pushes the impurities out of the lungs.

Breathing, activated by the dual current of prana and Apana, is physiologically accomplished through a series of complex nerve reflexes - chemical and mechanical - primarily involving the medulla oblongata and the sympathetic, or involuntary, nervous system. The intricate sympathetic system, in turn, is reinforced by the prana and Apana currents that work through the vital branches of the astral currents that correspond to the sympathetic nervous system - the main branches of which are called Ida and Pingala.

The study of the physiology of breathing without an appreciable understanding of the principles of the subtle life behind this is like studying Shakespeare's Hamlet, leaving out the parts that portray Hamlet's character.

Inspiration and exhalation work involuntarily through a life. As long as the vital current (prana) pushes inspiration into the lungs, man lives; whenever the downward current (Apana) in the exhalation becomes stronger, man dies. The Apana current then pushes the astral body out of the physical body. When the final breath leaves the body through the action of the outgoing current, Apana, the astral body, follows it to the astral world.

It is also said that the human breath binds the soul to the body. It is the process of expiration and inspiration resulting from the two opposite currents in the backbone that give man the external world's perception. Dual breathing is the storm that creates waves (sensations) in the lake of the mind. These sensations produce body consciousness and duality and also throw oblivion on the unified consciousness of the soul.

The Mystery of the Breath

God dreamed the soul and enclosed it in a dream body with a dream breath. The mystery of the breath brings with it the solution to the secret of human existence.

There is also a direct connection between breathing and physical longevity. The dog, for example, breathes quickly and therefore has a shorter life. The crocodile breathes very slowly and can live for over a hundred years.

Corpulent people breathe heavily and die prematurely. When the dream of breath vanishes through illness, old age, or other physical causes, the dream body's death follows.

Therefore, the Yogis reasoned that if the body did not decay and toxins did not accumulate in the cells, breathing would no longer be necessary; that scientific mastery of breathing that prevents decay in the body would make the flow of breath unnecessary and would give control over life and death. From this intuitive perception the ancient rishis created the science and art of prana - yama, life-control.

The Bhagavad Gita suggests the Pranayama as a universal method for humans to release the soul from the bondage of breath.

Check the currents of Prana and Apana

The Gita states: "The yogi is greater than the ascetics who discipline the body, greater than even those who follow the path of wisdom or the path of action; be a Yogi! " (VI: 46). This is the pranayama of Kriya Yoga to which we refer and is not only highlighted in this verse IV: 29, but also in V: 27-28: "Expert in meditation (muni) becomes free the one who, seeking the Supreme Goal, is able to withdraw from external phenomena by fixing attention at the point between the eyebrows and neutralizing the negative currents of prana and Apana - which flow - through the nostrils and lungs ...."

The ancient sage Patanjali, the most important exponent of Yoga, also speaks of the pranayama of Kriya Yoga: "Liberation can be achieved through that pranayama that is accomplished by disconnecting the course of inspiration with exhalation." (Yoga Sutra 11:49)

Breath, lungs, heart slowdown in sleep but are not completely blocked. But through Kriya Yoga the breath gradually subsides and the movements of the lungs and body are blocked. When motor movement leaves the whole body, possessing the lack of agitation and reaching mental and physical firmness, venous blood ceases to accumulate. Venous blood is ordinarily pumped from the heart into the lungs for purification, the heart and lungs are quiet. The breathing ceases to come and go from the lungs through the mechanical action of the diaphragm.

The pranayama Kriya Yoga stops the decay of the body associated to Apana poster exhalation, through the fresh oblation of vital force or prana, distilled from inspiration. This practice allows the devotee to dispel the illusion of growth and decay of the body as flesh; he therefore realizes that it is made of vitatrons.

The Kriya Yogi body is recharged with extra energy distilled from the breath and strengthened by the tremendous dynamo of energy generated in the spine; the decay of body tissues decreases. This decrease and ultimately makes the heart's function of cleaning the blood unnecessary. When the pulsating life pumped by the heart subsides, due to the non-pumping of the venous blood, exhalation and inspiration are no longer necessary. The life force, which had dissipated into cellular, nervous, respiratory and cardiac actions, converges from the senses and external organs and unites with the current in the spine.

The Kriya Yogi therefore learns how to mix the ascending stream of life (prana) into the descending stream (Apana) and mixing the descending stream (Apana) into the ascending stream (prana). He therefore neutralizes the dual movement, and through willpower brings both currents into a revealing spiritual sphere of light at the point between the eyebrows.

This light of pure vital energy sparkles from the cerebrospinal centres directly to all bodily cells, magnetizing them, stopping growth and decay, and making them self-sustained at the vital level, regardless of breathing or external sources of life.

As long as this light will flow up and down as the two current fighters of prana and Apana - inspiration and expiration - lend their life and light to sensory perceptions and the deadly processes of growth and decay.

But when the yogi can neutralize the upward and downward thrust of the spinal currents, and can carry all the life force from the senses and motor sensory nerves, and can keep the life force still at the point between the eyebrows, the brain light gives the yogi the vital control or power over prana (pranayama Kriya Yoga).

The senses' life force is concentrated in a fixed inner light in which the Spirit and His Cosmic Light is revealed.

The Pranayama Kriya Yoga, the science of breath neutralization method has nothing in common with silly practices that attempt to control the current of life by forcing the retention of breath in the lungs - a non-scientific practice, unnatural and dangerous. Anyone holding their breath for a few minutes in their lung's experiences panic, suffocation, and tension in the heart.

These adverse effects on the body should be sufficient proof that the yogi will not recommend such a practice. Some teachers advise unscientifically - not to mention that it is impossible - retention of breath in the lungs - a practice completely prohibited by the Illuminati yogis.

Yoga, the highest knowledge of the human being, is not a dogmatic cult or creed, but rather recommendations per se for the greatest scientists of the West and the East.

True Kumbhakar, or breath retention mentioned in the enlightened yoga treatises, does not refer to forcibly holding the breath in the lungs, but to the natural absence of breath acquired by scientific pranayama, which makes breathing no longer necessary.

At Kriya Yoga it has been referred crosswise in many yoga scriptures and treatises like Kavala Pranayama or Kavala Kumbhakar - the true pranayama or the vital control that transcends the need of inspiration (puraka) and exhalation (rechaka); breath is transmuted into currents of inner life force under complete control of the mind.

"When breathing stops effortlessly, without even rechaka (exhalation) or puraka (inspiration), this is called KevalaKumbhaka." - Hatha-Yoga Pradipika, 11:73.

"The aspirant who can perform Kevali Kumbhakar, who has no rechaka and puraka, he alone is the true connoisseur of Yoga." - Gheranda Samhita, v: 95.

"One who is expert in the Kavala Kumbhakar, which has no rechaka and puraka, will have nothing unattainable in the three worlds." - Siva Samhita 111: 46-47.

Of the various stages of breathless pranayama (kumbhaka), Kevali is exalted by expert yogis as the best or the highest. In principle, it can be equated with Kriya Yoga, Kevali Pranayama is not as explicit as the science and techniques of Kriya Yoga reported and clarified for this time by MahavatarBabaji and given to the world through LahiriMahasaya.

Chapter 14.   Kundalini Exercises

Just as with the yoga and meditation kundalini exercises, we must be confident that we are prepared for these practices. Approach these advanced exercises just as you have been with your routine, find your practice space, clear your mind, have an empty stomach, and overall be respectful of kundalini.

Kundalini should be approached with the utmost respect. You may even wish to leave an offering or prayer before your practice advances. As we begin these practices, let's keep in mind the power of the present moment. Just as a meditation practice aims to achieve, our mind is clearest in the present moment. We are the most attentive and efficient when we are at this moment. We need to maintain this focus when working with kundalini. She requires our attention and respect as we wake her. We do not want to startle her or anger her as we approach these techniques. We must be in the most attentive and focused state that we have ever experienced to achieve the results we seek,

One final note before the exercises begin: Listen to your body. If you do not feel that you are ready to approach kundalini, then absolutely do not do it! There is no shame in being honest with yourself about your practice. As we have mentioned throughout this book, not everyone will progress in the same way. We need to be honest with ourselves about our progress and be truthful when we ask ourselves if we are ready. For what it's worth, the more practice you have before approaching the serpent, the more likely you will be successful in your endeavors. Take your time and be patient. Hone your skills and have an enjoyable experience as you do. This is not a career or a job. There is no deadline or strict structure. Create your path by listening to your body and mind. You will intuitively know that you are ready when you are ready, do not approach kundalini until you are sure that you will be able to adhere to your promises to her.

Starting Out

As we mentioned, the present moment is key to these practices. Stay in this moment and do not worry about the past or future. If you can to stay in the present moment, you will begin to dissolve the deepest illusions your mind has constantly been creating about nature's true reality. You can start by seeing the reality of the endless energy of divine bliss in everyone and everything. This bliss is always there. We just need to see it. If we buy into the delusions of the chaotic mind at any moment, our kundalini working will have failed, and we will need to start over. This is very common, so do not be discouraged.

By staying consciously here in this eternal moment, the phenomena of psychic abilities, unseen powers, and magical manifestation will naturally begin to happen in your life. Combined with the practices in this book, we can optimize these powers. Kundalini will give you the capacity to attract anything in the world you desire. Since these practices act to merge the kundalini's infinite power with your subtle energetic and physical bodies, we effectively upgrade our existence. This upgrade may even protect us from emotional attacks or various otherworldly disasters.

As we are willing to live in this present moment, we will empower ourselves as individuals. With these kundalini workings, we can essentially tap into the source of the universe and keep it near throughout our lives. Sure, we can work with our chakras with kundalini still dormant, but to get the absolute most out of these practices, we will need kundalini to be awake, piercing our chakras and opening them fully to the universal power. When each of the seven chakra centers in your body is ignited, you will transverse the world as you know it. No longer bound to time or worry. The God and Goddess, Shiva and Shakti, within you will become very apparent, and you will know without a doubt that powers are inherent in your body and mind. From this point, there is no turning back, your life is altered completely, and you now are familiar with some secrets of the universe.

Practices

The following practices will combine what we have learned throughout this book. Meditation, yoga, mantra, and visualization is the key component of the following exercises. These practices are the most complex and challenging and are specifically designed for kundalini awakening.

Keep the serpent energy in mind as you practice these exercises. Visualize the dormant snake at the base of your spine. Imagine the infinite potential in the awakening of this energy that is a fiery spark of consciousness just waiting to rise inside you. As you take on these final practices, you will awake this energy. If you have put in the time and effort, you will build this relationship with kundalini. This energy may rise slowly or gradually make itself known, but there are many times that this energy bursts out of its slumber, rise aggressively through your spine. Many have described this feeling online and in spiritual communities. This flood of life is incredible and changes the lives of the experiencers forever. Raising this energy will essentially begin your new life; you will be living fully for the first time. There is an infinite potential of where to go from that point, eventually unifying Shakti and Shiva, allowing them to dance the creative expression of oneness through you.

Kundalini Exercise 1

This is a sequence of exercises that ignites the fire within in hopes of waking kundalini. The mantras used is related to the name of truth and acts to stimulate our entire being with its vibration. The yoga poses and visualization act to engage your energetic body as well as your physical body to really get the energy moving.

Practice these exercises after your body is sufficiently warmed up after some light yoga or breathing exercises.

1. Kneel onto your knees, sitting on the heels of your feet.

2. Inhale and bend forward, touching your brow to the ground

3. Breathe deeply for ten breaths, relaxing into the position.

4. Chant the following mantra, internally or out loud:

Sat, Sat, Sat, Sat, Sat, Sat, Naam.

As you chant, each Sat should be vibrated into a chakra, starting with the root and rising through the other chakras until we reach the crown chakra and chant Naam. Continue this exercise for ten minutes, then move onto the next step for Kundalini exercise 1.

After you have completed the Sat Naam exercise, you can begin the next sequence. This practice is simple and helps to relax after the Sat Naam practice.

5. Raise your brow from the floor.

6. Slowly stretch your legs outward, extending them in front of you.

7. Straighten your back and raise your hands above your head.

8. Bend at the hips and try to grab your toes; hold this position.

9. Breathe deeply for seven breaths.

Each of the seven breaths should engage a chakra. Visualize the breath penetrating the root chakra, then upward through the other chakras until your seventh breath. After the seventh breath, immediately move onto the next sequence.

This part of the exercise is a winding down of sorts. You will feel the energy in your body shift dramatically. Take note of the changes you experience as you relax.

10.   Raise up from touching your toes then lay down on your back.

11.   Relax your body with your hands at your sides. Breathe deeply.

12.   Lay here motionless for seven minutes.

As you lay quietly, visualize kundalini lying dormant. Not unlike your motionless body, she lays asleep. Visualize her as a literal snake, just let the details come as they will.

Once you have reached seven minutes, rise up slowly, visualizing kundalini awakening. Sit quietly with your visualization and see what happens. Sit quietly and breathe normally.

This is the end of the first kundalini exercise, but after you relaxed, you can perform it again and again. It is best not to perform this exercise more than three times per day.

Kundalini Exercise 2

This sequence of exercises is designed for purification of the body and chakras. It acts as an overall clearing and opening, making way for the kundalini energy to rise. This purification is much needed in a world of synthetic drugs and foods. This exercise pairs well after long work weeks or before healing baths.

1. Stand up straight, balancing your weight on our feet.

2. Stretch your leg behind you with the top of your foot staying on the ground.

3. Bend the other leg until you have a ninety-degree angle at your knee, your weight will be on the bent leg.

4. Place your palms together, and hold at your chest, focus your vision on your brow.

5. Deep breathe in this position.

6. Stand up and switch legs performing the same exercise.

This practice is a physical work out that helps to get the body moving and engage the chakras in preparation for the next sequence.

7. Sit down and cross your legs comfortably.

8. Put your hands on your hips and raise your diaphragm.

9. Breathe deeply in this position for three minutes.

The next sequence is more intensive, you can view the first sequences as a warm-up for the next ones.

10. Stay seated and breathing consistently.

11. Interlock your hands at your chest, forearms parallel to the floor.

12. Inhale as deep as you can.

13. Forcibly exhale all the breath as fast as you can.

14. Inhale fully and hold breath.

15. Exhale completely and forcibly.

16. Continue this practice for three minutes.

We should be raising the energy up through the chakras as we practice this, the forced breaths engaging the solar plexus chakra and heart chakra. The next sequence contacts the throat and third eye chakras.

17.   Stay seated with your legs crossed.

18.   Extend the arms out at the sides like wings.

19.   Roll your eyes up gazing at your brow.

20.   Breathe deeply and hold this position for 3 minutes.

21.   Press your hands together and straighten your spine.

22.   Push firm on your hands and hold this position for three minutes.

This exercise is excellent for purification purposes but also works directly with kundalini energy. Visualizing kundalini being purified with this practice can add to the potency as well.

Exercise for Blockages

This exercise is great for clearing blockages in your chakras and nadis. It acts as a great precursor to kundalini works while also engaging the kundalini. Practice this exercise on a weekly basis. It ensures your chakras do not become clogged.

1. Sit with your legs crossed and raise your hands over your head. Practice a range of motion, stretching your arms in circles.

2. Clinch your fists at your heart and roll your shoulders forward and backward.

This exercise becomes quite fun as you move through the steps quickly. It can almost become a dance of sorts. This exercise can be performed before an intensive yoga or meditation session to get the energy flowing smoothly.

A Note on Ancestral Lineage

This exercise is great for breaking ancestral blockages as well. Consider all the people in your ancestral line, only a small fraction of them that you have met. These lines can get blocked just as energetic channels get blocked by day-to-day life. There may be criminals or other troublemakers in this lineage.

The advanced techniques of working to clear our energetic ancestral lineage are powerful and complex. Use the blockage exercises above to heal your ancestral lines visually. You can imagine the line of ancestors going all the way back to the source of consciousness, healing it along the way. You may even want to leave offerings or call upon your ancestors to assist you in this work.

Ancestral practices are very complex and would need a whole book to explore properly. For now, use the blockage techniques to clear your family line.

Chakra Balancing Exercise

Stimulating the chakra system at least once per day is good practice to ensure that your chakras will not become blocked or unbalanced in the future. Deep breathing exercises and a consistent yoga routine go a long way to achieve this balanced system, but we also must practice more intensive exercises, especially if we have yet to awaken the kundalini energy.

1. In a standing position, place your feet shoulder-width apart.

2. Squat down so the thighs are parallel to the floor.

3. Reach towards your toes; placing the palms on top of the feet, be sure to keep your back straight.

4. Lift your head and look forward.

5. Move to a kneeling position, sit on the heels, and stretch the arms straight over your head.

6. Interlock your fingers except for the index fingers, which should be pointing straight up.

7. Begin to chantSat Naam' emphatically in a constant rhythm.

8. On Naam, relax the stomach.

9. Continue for three minutes.

This exercise is great for stimulating the entire chakra system. The second section continues this practice. If you wish to practice the above before moving on to the second sequence, then do so until you are fully prepared to perform the entire exercise. This is your practice, so make it what you want and go at your own pace.

10. Kneel sitting on your heels, rest the hands on the thighs.

11. Begin inhaling in short sips through your pursed lips until the lungs are full of air.

12. With your breath held, raise up and rotate the hips around in a circle.

13. Exhale and sit back down on your heels.

14. Move to a lying position and bring the hands to the Navel Point. The left hand is closest to the body, and the right hand is over the left.

This is a great exercise for learning to feel the chakras as well. Step 16 is essentially asking you to use your hands in circular motions to feel and manipulate the chakras. Move on with the next steps after you have sufficiently felt and moved the chakras.

15. Remain on your back and extend your arms straight above you.

16. Make fists of your hands and pull your fists into your chest.

17. Release your clenched fists and repeat three more times.

18. Resting on your back, place the left hand on the heart and the right hand over the left.

19. Breathe deeply and engage your heart chakra.

20. Release your fists and place your hands at your sides.

21. Lay comfortably for five to ten minutes.

This exercise acts to clear away chakra blockages while also acting as a great warm-up exercise to start your day or begin your kundalini practices. These complex exercises have so many steps because this is the effort needed to stimulate the kundalini energy.

The kundalini exercises above are the methods that will skyrocket your practice from a humble beginner's practice to a full-fledged advanced routine. When these exercises are practiced consistently and approached with respect and seriousness, you will surely open your chakras and awaken the kundalini energy. These practices should all be performed on an empty stomach to avoid cramps or indigestion. This is why we recommend performing them in the morning when you first awake. Your belly will be empty, and you will have a fresh canvas to work with as you start your day. Not to mention these exercises get the blood moving; you may even be able to skip your coffee!

Conclusion

As we walk around each day, we are in a constant state of energetic vibration. You might feel this when you're in a crowded room, and you're feeling "off" or "uncomfortable."You feel this way because the energy of the room is compromising your energy. For us, Third Eye Awakening means the feeling of being in the flow. It's that moment when you completely lose yourself in a task or an activity, when you're on and in the zone. That feeling of being in the flow is really important for us because it's when we feel most alive.

Kundalini Awakening And Crystals can help you to activate the power of crystals. You can start by holding them, meditating on them, and setting intentions for them. Then, you can make elixirs with them and wear them as jewelry.

One of the most powerful things you can do to start your journey to more spiritual life is to start meditating and connecting with your higher self. The first step to meditation is to start by clearing your mind. This is where crystals can help. There are many different kinds of crystals, and one of the most powerful of these is the quartz crystal. Third Eye Awakening is a natural energy that is an essential part of the human experience. It's something we all possess, but most people aren't aware of it. In Kundalini Awakening And Crystals, the Kundalini is the serpent that lies at the base of the spine. It is said to be coiled energy, which lies dormant until it is awakened.

The next step upon successful completion of this book is to of course, practice and apply what you have learned. Practice and application always go hand in hand in retaining the information that one has learned. Without practice, the skills that you learned from this book will never be enhanced and be cultivated. Try to quiz yourself if you know the uses of the different crystals. Try to match the sickness with the appropriate crystals that can cure them. Try to find the location of your chakra without looking at a guide. Try the simple and different ways of cleansing your crystals. Try and practice until you have mastered the craft of crystal healing because that will be the only true way of succeeding.

May you also pass on to others the techniques and the knowledge about the art of crystal healing you have learned in this book. I hope you can inspire others to learn and appreciate this kind of alternative therapy as much as this book has encouraged. Remember to always learn and learn no matter how knowledgeable you become in crystal healing, for there will always be new and available information waiting for you to discover. A great crystal healer will never stop researching and learning all about his or her craft.

Printed in Great Britain
by Amazon